MY STORIES, MY TIMES
VOLUME 2

MY STORIES, MY TIMES

VOLUME 2

JEAN CHRÉTIEN

TRANSLATED BY
SHEILA FISCHMAN
AND DONALD WINKLER

RANDOM HOUSE CANADA

PUBLISHED BY RANDOM HOUSE CANADA

Published simultaneously in French as *Mes nouvelles histoires*
by Éditions La Presse, Montreal.

www.penguinrandomhouse.ca

Library and Archives Canada Cataloguing in Publication

Title: My stories, my times. Volume 2 / Jean Chrétien ; translated by
Sheila Fischman and Donald Winkler.
Names: Chrétien, Jean, 1934- author.
Description: Translated from the original French.
Identifiers: Canadiana (print) 20210207051 | Canadiana (ebook) 2021020706X |
ISBN 9781039000971 (hardcover) | ISBN 9781039000995 (EPUB)
Subjects: LCSH: Chrétien, Jean, 1934-—Anecdotes. | LCSH: Prime ministers—
Canada—Anecdotes. | CSH: Canada—Politics and government—1963-1984. |
CSH: Canada—Politics and government—1984-1993. | CSH: Canada—Politics
and government—1993-2006. | LCGFT: Anecdotes.
Classification: LCC FC636.C47 A3 2021 | DDC 971.064/8092—dc23

Text design: Andrew Roberts
Jacket design: Andrew Roberts

Printed in Canada

10 9 8 7 6 5 4 3 2 1

Penguin
Random House
RANDOM HOUSE CANADA

For Aline, the one and only, the love of my life and my Rock of Gibraltar, who left us too soon.

CONTENTS

FOREWORD BY ROY ROMANOW

O ne of the many rewards of political life is the extraordinary individuals you meet along the way, and the
unexpected friendships that grow out of circumstances. It's
always an occasion when such a friend has written a new book,
and I am honoured to have the opportunity to set down some
reminiscences of the era when events brought me together
with the future "Monseiur le Premier Ministre," Jean Chrétien.

In the late 1970s, during his third term as prime minister,
Pierre Trudeau went on the road with a mission: to meet with
all of the nation's premiers to garner their support for the
patriation of the British North America Act from Westminster
to Canada. At the time when Mr. Trudeau came to Regina to
meet with then Premier Allan Blakeney, I was deputy premier and attorney general of Saskatchewan, and so my premier
asked me to attend the meeting.

Prime Minister Pierre Trudeau was an impressive and
intelligent leader who by now had a great deal of experience
with the complexities of governance in Canada. Trudeau's
main argument in favour of patriation was that Canada was

an independent nation and he wished to have this fact established, clearly and finally. As well, he proposed that a patriated constitution should include new amendments to reflect modern-day Canada.

Of course, one vital issue gave Trudeau's national project a particular degree of urgency: the growing momentum of the nationalist movement in Quebec. With a separatist government in place, led by the formidable premier René Lévesque, Trudeau knew time was of the essence. The prime minister proposed that Ottawa and the provinces establish a working committee of ministers and officials to work out the details of the new "Canada Act."

And so, after the Quebec referendum in June 1980, Jean Chrétien, as federal minister of justice, and I as the attorney general of Saskatchewan, became the co-chairs of the Continuing Committee of Ministers on the Constitution (CCMC). It was not the first time that Jean Chrétien and I had dealings with each other—our paths had crossed from time to time with matters related to justice department affairs. But our new co-chair responsibilities would bring us together at a unique time and place at our country's history, and cement lasting bonds of friendship.

The CCMC was composed of about 250 officials representing all provinces and territories. With national hearings held in every province, there was growing public interest in the enterprise. Each provincial delegation aired their own specific concerns, ranging from fishing rights in the Atlantic provinces to jurisdictional control over natural resources in

Alberta and Saskatchewan. But by far, the issue that dominated the discussions was the Parti Québécois government's fundamental desire to break away from the federation, which posed obvious difficulties during a process that sought to achieve federal–provincial harmony.

No matter what transpired in sessions behind closed doors, Jean Chrétien and I always made it a point to meet with the press each day after our closed hearings and arguments with provincial and territorial governments had concluded. The Ottawa media gallery saw fit to dub these briefings "The Uke and Tuque show"—a nod to my Ukrainian background and to Mr. Chrétien's home province of Quebec.

In these exciting and extremely challenging circumstances, I got to know Jean Chrétien quite well. No matter how tough a working session of the CCMC was, Jean Chrétien always maintained a confident and positive approach to our mission, namely, to arm our First Ministers and the public with the facts in support of unity while describing the grave danger of a national break-up of our country. He was extremely perceptive of the Quebec government's ultimate motivation, which was to withdraw from the Canadian confederation. Jean was chief among those who truly believed that Quebecers needed to know just how final and damaging separation would be to both Quebec and Canada. Some of the most eloquent and passionate debates took place between Chrétien and his Quebec challengers.

The four-day First Ministers' conference that began in Ottawa on November 2, 1981 brought us all together "one last time" to try to make patriation a reality. Three days in, progress was stalled, with Ontario and New Brunswick siding with Prime Minister Trudeau and the "Gang of Eight" provinces still not convinced. When formal talks broke off that day, Jean Chrétien approached me and said, "We've got to get together quickly." We located a small kitchenette in the National Conference Centre and set down some points based on notes we had exchanged with the Ontario Attorney General Roy McMurtry earlier in the day. We pulled Roy into the room, and within about ten minutes, we had drafted on two sheets of paper the handwritten notes that would become known to posterity as "The Kitchen Accord." It was then Roy's and my job to sell the proposition to the provincial leaders. It was Jean's job to sell it to Pierre Trudeau—and he has always maintained his was the more difficult assignment!

It is a testament to Jean Chrétien's persistence and creativity that we found a way to a deal that day, even though Quebec did not sign on. Pierre Trudeau had said that if there was anyone who could find a way to a deal it was Jean. His boss trusted his skills not just as a negotiator but as someone who was always ready and willing to work across party lines. (And it's interesting to note that the Kitchen Accord details were hammered out amongst a Progressive Conservative, a Liberal, and a member of the New Democratic Party.)

Years later, as the political gods would have it, both Jean Chrétien and I would have a different sort of working relationship when Jean was elected to the position of prime minister and myself as premier of Saskatchewan. We certainly had our differences over resource revenue distribution and interpretations of what the renewed constitution intended. But having served together during such a serious test of Canadian unity, we knew as well as anyone the value of cooperation. Our friendship, mutual respect and joint admiration for Canada led us to fair and reasonable compromises.

Over his long career in public service, Jean Chrétien developed a profound understanding of the challenges inherent in governing a vast nation with two official languages and great regional disparities, and the compromises and accommodations that are necessary to govern effectively and envision progress for all citizens. This new book is a testament to his continued commitment to a prosperous and fair Canada. A skillful negotiator whose intellect and determination proved vital at times of grave importance to the country's unity, Jean Chrétien remains one of our great prime ministers. Told with insight, honesty, and a good amount of humour, these stories illustrate the challenges and the triumphs of politics, and the many lessons learned during a lifetime of outstanding public service. Few understand Canada and Canadians more than he does.

Roy Romanow, PC, OC, SOM, QC

PREFACE

It is with great pleasure that I take up my pen once more to continue our conversation, because I have not yet told all my stories. Once I promised my grandchildren that I would write them down, I found that I was enjoying myself, and so here are some more. After the first volume of *My Stories, My Times* was published in October 2018, I went back to my desk, in silence, and alone with my pen and my memories, far from the discouraging racket of the news incessantly beamed to us from our neighbours to the south, exposing us to the ravings of a rudderless president.

In addition to that, I was obliged by health concerns to spend the month of August 2019 immobilized, my left arm in a sling, at my summer home at Lac des Piles. No golf, no swimming, no walking in the woods; nothing to distract me and plenty of time to write. What's more, as I compose these lines, I haven't left my house for more than eighty days. It's more restful to set down words than to monitor from morning to night the chronicling of the COVID-19 pandemic and its ravages.

This book is a bit different from the one that came out in the autumn of 2018, because while writing these accounts, I have paid particular attention to the intersection of the present with the past.

In the course of my long career, journalists, editorial writers, and observers of all kinds have made every sort of comment imaginable and used every adjective in the dictionary to assess my performance. But there came a day when one of them, finding himself short of words or ideas, declared that I had never read a book in my life. No doubt he'd be taken aback to learn that this is the fourth book I've written. During my active life in politics, if someone had said that one day I would find myself writing a fourth book, I'd have burst out laughing. Truthfully, I had never envisaged such a possibility. Let me tell you how it came about that I made my entry into the world of scribes, and what led me to write my first book, *Straight from the Heart*.

Having been a member of the cabinets of Lester B. Pearson and Pierre Elliott Trudeau; having served in eight important ministerial positions; having been responsible under the Trudeau government for the 1980 referendum dossier, the repatriation of the Constitution, and the embedding of the Charter of Rights and Freedoms; I had acquired a certain notoriety, all of which led Anna Porter, the eponymous publisher of Toronto's Key Porter Books, to contact me. After discussing my political career, she told me that she wanted me to write a book.

I replied that I wasn't a writer, and that I wasn't interested. "Monsieur Chrétien, you're going to write a book!" I retorted, "No, Madame, I will not write a book." She kept insisting, and I told her, "A politician writes a book because he wants to explain himself, and I have nothing to explain." Anna Porter is clearly a woman who doesn't give up easily, and she persevered. So I explained to her that to write a book, you need a big ego, and mine was already big enough for my purposes, thank you. She repeated, "Monsieur Chrétien, you're going to write a book!" and I again responded, "No, Madame Porter, I am not writing a book." So then she wrote a cheque and I wrote a book . . .

It was a great success. In her own book *In Other Words*, Anna Porter wrote, "The book sold more than 200,000 copies in English and maybe half that in French." And further on: "On the heels of our overwhelming success with *Straight from the Heart*, Key Porter won the 'Publisher of the Year' Award from the Canadian Booksellers Association." And so if it weren't for Anna Porter, you would not now be reading these lines.

As a student at Laval in Quebec City, I was already president of the university's Young Liberals at age twenty-two, and I participated in the 1956 provincial election. The member of the legislative assembly I was supporting, René Hamel, was leader of the Opposition during the Duplessis regime, and minister of justice under Jean Lesage. Standing by his side, I gave more than twelve speeches, which made him my first teacher. This sixty-four-year journey has enabled me to follow the progress that we've made over more than half a century.

Despite all our detours, at times unnerving, at others frankly discouraging, we've always survived the storms that have on occasion troubled our country's political life. That is why I hope that the time you'll spend reading my stories will leave you with the sense that when all's said and done, our political system, however imperfect it may be, has no reason to envy that of any other country.

1

EVEN IN RETIREMENT

At the urging of many readers who seem to have appreciated these varied and brief accounts, I am once again recounting some tales that offer a backstage view of political life. As I'm in pretty good shape despite my venerable eighty-five years, I'm having another go at it, though with no guarantee that another book will result. I'm advised that sequels are rarely as successful as an initial book. Could be, but I tell myself that if this opportunity to write ends up producing a book that's less popular than the first, so be it! I'll still have had the pleasure of spending long, peaceful hours at my work table, reliving episodes from my forty years of public life.

September 2019. Even though I'm retired, it's impossible for me to say no when I'm asked to make a contribution to public life—but sometimes I go a bit too far, as was the case last week, for example.

A month ago, our ambassador to the United Nations, Marc-André Blanchard, asked me to help prepare for the opening of the General Assembly, on September 23. I agreed to grant him three days out of the five he had asked for, because I already had professional commitments in British Columbia for the Thursday and Friday of that week. And so on September 23, I got up at 3:30 a.m. to catch the first plane out of Ottawa to New York. The ambassador had prepared a rather heavy schedule for me, and over three days, I had to participate in bilateral meetings with heads of state and government, with ministers and ambassadors. During those few days, I tallied no fewer than twenty-five different meetings to promote Canada's candidature for a non-permanent seat on the United Nations Security Council.

The stakes were very high for Justin Trudeau's Liberal government, since for the first time in our history, the Harper government had lost the vote in 2010, which was seen as a diplomatic humiliation for Canada and its Conservative prime minister. At the time of this defeat, I'd met in New York a former American president and a former prime minister of Portugal, who had expressed surprise at seeing their countries outstrip Canada in that race. I told them that things would have been different had my party been in power.

In fact, in 1998 my government had won that seat in the first round, with a substantial majority. We have to assume that the Harper government's aggressive attitude toward China, Russia, and the Palestinians, and our withdrawal from the African continent contrasted with our successful initiatives, including the Ottawa Convention on the banning of anti-personnel mines, the establishment of the International

Court of Justice, the request on the part of my G8 colleagues that we assume responsibility on their behalf for the New Partnership for Africa's Development (NEPAD), and so on. I must say that I was impressed by the quality of the work done by Ambassador Blanchard and his team, but it was clear that we had not completely recovered from our decline on the international stage, which had occurred between 2006 and 2015. I feared, unfortunately, that our results would be very problematical once the votes were counted, in June of 2020. (And so it turned out, as Canada failed to win back a seat on the Security Council.)

After I'd finished my work at the United Nations, I took a plane on Wednesday evening for Vancouver. I participated in three political meetings to support the Liberal MPs and candidates in the run-up to the election of October 21, 2019. I must say that I did not find the mood as electric as during Justin Trudeau's first campaign in 2015. Following my exchanges with the candidates, supporters, and journalists, I concluded that the Liberals would lose seats in British Columbia. How many? It was hard to say, three weeks before the end of the campaign.

The next day, I travelled to Kelowna in the beautiful Okanagan Valley, where for eighty minutes I answered questions posed by veteran journalist Kent Molgat before an audience of 1,200 businesspeople. Molgat was very well prepared, and his questions were to the point, which enabled me to do a good job. The crowd reacted enthusiastically, and I was happy to see that, at the age of eighty-five, I could still keep out of trouble quite easily.

I readily agreed to lend a hand to Liberal candidates, one of whom was already an MP. I believe that the member Stephen Fuhr of Kelowna was the first Liberal elected in this riding for fifty years. I was impressed by his energy and his ease, and also by the many supporters on his campaign committee. There was a winning atmosphere surrounding the young member. It's not easy for a Liberal to win a seat in the British Columbia interior. But in this riding, I thought it was possible.

My political duties fulfilled, I went for a drink with Senator Ross Fitzpatrick, a friend I'd met in Ottawa in 1965, when he was assistant to the then labour minister John Robert Nicholson. What a surprise to meet there two old cronies: Herb Dhaliwal, who was an excellent minister in my cabinet, and the first Indo-Canadian to be in that position; and lawyer Louis Salley, an Alberta francophone who had made a brilliant career in Vancouver. Also present at the gathering was Gordon, Senator Fitzpatrick's son, who had worked for me when I was the minister of energy, mines, and resources from 1982 to 1984. After this most agreeable social interlude, dominated by intense exchanges concerning the upcoming federal elections, I returned to my hotel to spend a short night before flying from Kelowna to Calgary, then to Ottawa, where I arrived on Saturday night. The next day, I made my way to Montreal to take off for Paris in order to attend the funeral of Jacques Chirac, the former French president, and my colleague on the international scene from 1995 to 2003.

Arriving in Paris the next day at six in the morning, after a shower and breakfast I headed for the French Senate, where the dignitaries gathered before boarding a bus bound for the Saint-Sulpice church. As we waited, I was able to greet several acquaintances from my political life. Canada was represented by Governor General Julie Payette and myself, and Quebec by two former premiers, Lucien Bouchard and Jean Charest. They were two former political adversaries: Bouchard as leader of the Bloc Québécois in 1993, and Jean Charest as leader of the Progressive Conservatives in 1997. On the other hand, Charest and I had worked well together during the 1995 referendum, and we had made Bouchard bite the dust following that famous confrontation in Quebec.

And yet, there we were, the three of us in Paris, and despite our differences and the tough battles of the past, we had a very civilized conversation—I would say even pleaseant. When I found myself in the church along with Julie Payette, we were seated near two people that I knew well: Bill Clinton and Vladimir Putin. I introduced our Governor General to President Putin, with whom she chatted in Russian to his delighted surprise. Bill Clinton was even more surprised. And as a Canadian, I was very proud. Madame Payette had learned the language during her career as an astronaut, when she worked alongside Russian astronauts.

As the historic Notre-Dame de Paris Cathedral was not available due to the famous fire that partly ravaged it in April of 2019, the religious ceremony took place in the very beautiful and ancient Saint-Sulpice church near Les Invalides.

I'm always very moved to find myself in a place so majestic and charged with history as is that famous church. What a labour of sweat, sacrifice, and determination, decade after decade, it must have taken for the hundreds of workers to erect such a splendid monument. When they left this earth for a better world, they did not think we would remember them centuries later. They did not build such masterpieces for an immediate reward, but to serve and to help their faith in God to endure. We remain grateful to them today.

In this church that was full to bursting, and with thousands of French people outside, come to pay homage to a great public figure who served his country for more than a half-century, what struck me most was the simplicity of the Catholic service, punctuated by an excellent sermon on faith, the family, and public service. No tributes from family, friends, or comrades in arms, or from French authorities. Just a beautiful sermon, not too long. But there was music— and what music! With a wonderful choir. And Schubert, played on the piano by the great virtuoso Daniel Barenboim. On the church's front bench, Jacques Chirac's devoted daughter Claude and those dear to her took their places. Everything was simple, beautiful, and worthy of the man who had just left us.

After the ceremony, President Emmanuel Macron offered a lunch at the Élysée for a number of heads of state and former leaders such as myself. I must confess that it was most agreeable to find myself on the French president's home ground, a pleasure I had had over a period of ten years under the presidencies of François Mitterrand and Jacques Chirac.

I was most grateful to have been present for the farewell to my friend Jacques Chirac, whose career in public life remains exceptional. After serving in the French army, he was successively a *député*, minister, prime minister under two French presidents, mayor of Paris, and president of the French Republic for twelve years. During this long odyssey, he showed himself to be a great strategist, a hard fighter, a tough adversary, a politician always very close to his constituents, and a learned citizen who was excellent company. Our exchanges in the beginning were rather contentious, but the twenty last years saw the growth of a cordial friendship, steadfast and respectful. He was certainly the European I knew best and for whom I always had great respect.

Back in the hotel, I made an unusual acquaintance. Our Governor General received a visit from another astronaut, who had also been a minister in Jacques Chirac's cabinet. Madame Claudie Haigneré was accompanied by her husband, Jean-Pierre, also an astronaut, and I had the privilege of chatting with these distinguished scientists for an hour. It was fascinating.

Afterwards, I went to a restaurant with the former U.S. president Bill Clinton. For the occasion, he had invited a former French minister of health and foreign affairs, Philippe Douste-Blazy. Monsieur Douste-Blazy now works with foundations, including that of the Clintons, which deal with health issues in poor countries.* Clinton was surprised to learn that this former minister in the French government had spent two years at the Montreal Clinical Research Institute, and that his mentor was my younger brother, Michel, then director of this renowned research centre.

After a pleasant dinner during which we discussed medical research, health in developing countries, and obviously Donald Trump and American politics, I retired to my hotel. The next day, I boarded a plane once more to return to Canada. When I got home, Aline told me that I seemed very tired. No surprise: I had travelled to New York, Vancouver, Kelowna, Montreal, Paris, and Ottawa in only nine days and worked from morning to night. As they say in Mauricie, not too bad for a guy who's eighty-five.

---

*   Professor Philippe Douste-Blazy is a cardiologist who was minister of health in France, minister of foreign affairs, and under-secretary-general at the United Nations. He founded Unitaid, an international NGO that joined forces with the Clinton Foundation to make affordable medications to combat AIDS, tuberculosis, and malaria in developing countries.

2

DON MACDONALD

This chapter is devoted to a man who was certain to be prime minister. For ten days, everyone thought that he would become the leader of the Liberal Party and that he would defeat the Conservative government in February 1980. He would have been a great prime minister had Pierre Trudeau not changed his mind in December 1979.

On November 21, 1979, as soon as Pierre Trudeau announced that he was abandoning the leadership of the Liberal Party, rumour had it that John Turner would be his logical successor. The name of Donald (Don) Macdonald, former minister of finance, energy and resources, and other important departments, and who was considered the intellectual equal of Trudeau on the anglophone side of the party, was also on many lips, especially among those close to Trudeau. As Turner and Macdonald were no longer MPs, eyes turned toward the House of Commons, and the names of Jean Chrétien, Allan MacEachen, Don Johnston, and John Roberts were also among those mentioned.

At the beginning of December, to everyone's surprise, the overall favourite, John Turner, announced that he would not be a candidate. And so Don Macdonald became the logical favourite in his place, given his remarkable personality, his intelligence, and his vast experience. As soon as I arrived on Parliament Hill in April 1963, I quickly developed a friendship with the young Toronto MP. We often ate together, and our conversations were rather unusual, because I did not speak much English and he expressed himself as best he could in the language of Molière. Don corrected my mistakes and talked to me in French, and I helped him to correct his own errors. As we were not very satisfied with the progress we were making in the other official language, he accused me of being a bad French teacher, and I replied that it was rather the case that he was a poor student. In return, I accused him of being a bad English teacher, and he retorted that I was a terrible student.

When we played squash, he counted the points in French, and I did likewise in English. We were really very good friends. In the autumn of 1967, after having been elected three times as the member for Rosedale in 1962, 1963, and 1965, he confided to me that he was soon to inform his riding association that he would not be a candidate in the next election. I begged him to wait until 1968, because I thought that Prime Minister Pearson was soon going to be retiring from public life. And so Don did not at that time announce his pending withdrawal from politics. As predicted, Pearson resigned, and Don Macdonald became one of the key ministers under Trudeau until 1977. I then replaced him as Canadian finance minister when he left politics after fifteen years in the House of Commons.

When, on December 13, 1979, the Progressive Conservative Party's budget was defeated, Prime Minister Joe Clark submitted his government's resignation to the Governor General, and called an election. Ten days before this fateful moment, Don Macdonald had told Pierre Elliott Trudeau that he was accepting his suggestion that he be a candidate for his succession, and had informed his law firm partners that he would soon be leaving them.

The defeat of Clark's finance minister John Crosbie's budget and the scheduling of an election for February 18, 1980, forty-nine days later, left the Liberals leaderless, as the convention that would choose a replacement for Pierre Elliott Trudeau had been set for later in the spring. The Liberal Party executive decided to hold a quick convention in January to find a successor to the retiring leader. As John Turner had announced that he would not be a candidate, everyone agreed that given the urgency of the situation, Don Macdonald would be crowned leader of the Liberal Party. The vast majority of political observers were convinced that the Liberals would beat the Conservatives in the February 1980 election, and that Don Macdonald would then become prime minister of Canada.

Don phoned me to ask if I was going to run against him in January. I burst out laughing and said, "Are you crazy,

Don? I wouldn't stand a chance of beating you." "I know," he replied, "because people will say that it's an Anglo's turn. But I don't like the idea of being crowned party chief. You're very popular with the Liberals, and a short campaign, one against the other, would add some spice to the process. Also, after the convention, you could become my lieutenant." I told him that he was the de facto leader in my mind, and that I would consider his proposal.

Suddenly, to everyone's surprise, we were being launched into a general election without a leader. Some were pleased with the inevitable, predictable arrival of Don Macdonald, but others were ill at ease and felt that the best solution would be to persuade Trudeau to withdraw his resignation and remain party leader. One night, I was called to a meeting at the office of Treasury Board President Bob Andras. There were six ministers present, and we agreed that Trudeau should not come back, that he had done enough for the country. He had young children, he was highly praised for his exceptional career, and we felt that we had no right to ask him for any greater sacrifice. Among the members of this group, Marc Lalonde, very close to Trudeau, said that he had expressed similar sentiments to the retired leader, and we all agreed to follow his lead and individually share our feelings with Prime Minister Trudeau.

During this time, many other former ministers and members, led by Allan MacEachen, were putting pressure on Trudeau, urging him to withdraw his resignation and lead us into the next election, less than seven weeks away. Over five crucial days, Trudeau entertained visitors at his office or at the Opposition leader's home, but he made no public declaration. Imagine all the hubbub amongst the journalists, MPs, former ministers, and members of the Liberal Party executive during this short period!

As I had agreed to share my views with Trudeau, I phoned him on Friday and Saturday, but he only called back on Sunday night. He was to announce his decision the next morning. Having participated in the discussions around Ottawa, I knew that most of the people involved wanted the former prime minister to return. And so when I received his phone call on Sunday evening, I suspected that he was going to come back. I felt I was in quite a tricky position. What could I say to him? I manoeuvred in the following way: "Pierre, I know this is a difficult decision for you to make, and here is my opinion: Don't feel obliged to return. You have served the country and the party well. You don't owe anybody anything. Stay with your young children, if that's what you want. But if you're mad for politics like me, you're going to return, we're going to work hard, and I'm sure you'll win the election in February." Fourteen hours later, he withdrew his resignation, took the party in hand once more, and on February 18, 1980, won his fifth election since 1968.

In December 1979, poor Don Macdonald had to do an about-face, telling his family that he was not returning to politics, and his law partners that he was resuming his practice. And so he who was legitimately seen to be assuming the position of prime minister of the country in February 1980 simply went back to private life. Public life is sometimes cruel. I am sure that he would have been an excellent prime minister.

3

THE CHINESE PROBLEM

It was January 29, 2019, at the height of the diplomatic crisis between Canada and China following the arrest of the daughter of the founder of China's largest telecommunications company, Huawei, on December 1, 2018.

As soon as the arrest became a big national and international story, my telephone started ringing off the hook, and I saw that the situation was very serious. I was asked to intervene, because it was conceivable that things could become catastrophic for many people. After having discussed the problem with interested parties and with clients, I contacted Prime Minister Justin Trudeau's right-hand man, Gerry Butts, and shared my unease, along with that of a number of people who had communicated with me. He listened very politely and told me not to be concerned, that he would look into it on Monday and would get back to me. I was left waiting for his call, and I remained uncomfortable with his lack of concern. But I said to myself, "Why should I fret? It's not my problem after all, but that of the government."

Three days later, on December 11, 2018, I was in a Porter aircraft bound for Toronto, because I had meetings scheduled for the following day. I was in seat 2D. Suddenly, there arrived in seat 2A Chrystia Freeland, at the time minister of foreign affairs. As seats 2B and 2C were free, I sat beside Ms. Freeland, who found herself positioned between the window and myself. And so we had the opportunity to talk for more than an hour, and of course, we covered a lot of ground.

Obviously, we were able to discuss the Huawei executive Meng Wanzhou, who had not yet been released on bail and was still in prison. Ms. Freeland was quick to admit that this was a serious situation, that President Trump had created a fine mess for us, that we had to break the impasse as soon as possible, and finally, if I had any ideas, she would be pleased to hear from me. It was a very agreeable eighty-minute conversation, in the course of which we broached many subjects, from the United States to China, by way of Saudi Arabia, Russia, France, Brexit, and so on.

I was happy to offer my views, and I hoped that our exchange would be of some use. Minister Freeland recognized that Meng Wanzhou had to be rapidly released from prison so that she could return to China as soon as possible, and she asked me to pass on any suggestions that might aid the government. With my friend and former close collaborator Eddie Goldenberg, I came up with a few ideas, which we sent to the minister, but we never received so much as an acknowledgement. A request for a further meeting was also met with silence.

On Friday, December 21, I was able to contact Prime Minister Justin Trudeau to share my concerns and let him know that I thought it was wrong to claim that this was simply a question of law. In effect, President Donald Trump had himself turned the situation into a political problem by saying that if he were to obtain a satisfying commercial agreement with China, he would withdraw the charge against Meng Wanzhou. Mr. Trudeau then told me that John Bolton, the national security adviser, had informed him before December 1 of the U.S. government's intentions. Therefore, he was going to honour the rule of law and would never give in to the Chinese blackmail surrounding the arrest of the two Canadians Michael Kovrig and Michael Spavor. He made it a question of principle, with no regard for the consequences. He would go head-to-head with the Chinese, because he was a true defender of human rights, and so on.

Hanging up, I was quite simply dumbfounded. So Justin Trudeau's father and myself, during the twenty years we maintained relations with China, would have had no principles and would not have acted as defenders of human rights? While Pierre as prime minister and myself as minister of justice had given Canadians the Charter of Rights and Freedoms? What is more, during the fifteen private talks I had with the Chinese president Jiang Zemin, I systematically raised the question of human rights. I was also the first foreign leader to deliver a speech on human rights in China before the students of the

University of Beijing. And I did the same before the Association of Chinese Judges in Shanghai.

At the end of December, I got a call from a highly placed Chinese individual asking if I would be prepared to help resolve the impasse between our two countries. We talked on the phone a dozen times, and I proposed a solution that would respect the rule of law. Here it is: As the two Canadians are still in prison, if the Chinese were to allow them parole, as is the case for Meng Wanzhou in Canada, we could allow the two Canadians to return to Canada while awaiting their trial, and do the same for Ms. Meng. If the three promised to return home at the risk of losing their bail money, all would conform to the rule of law. As a Vancouver judge had said a few days earlier, it will take years before all the hearings at all levels of the appeal procedure will be heard in Canada. Which is to say that Ms. Meng could not be deported to the United States for two or three years.

When I was prime minister, we had a case in which the Chinese demanded the extradition of one of its citizens. President Jiang Zemin promised that the man would not be put to death, and I believe that the procedures leading up to the deportation lasted about four years. On Monday, January 29, 2019, I was asked if there was a real possibility that the Canadian government would accept this proposal, which respected in every sense the rule of law, because in any case the deportation of Meng Wanzhou to the United States could not take place before 2022, which showed that the U.S. government had not chosen the most efficient path toward laying its hands on their Chinese target. The answer was clear and unequivocal: absolutely not! No need for me; the situation was under control.

Despite this blunt refusal, I felt that I had done my humble duty, and as we say in Quebec, *j'ai pris mon trou*—I went back to my burrow. On this Sunday, February 3, as I write, I can see where Canada stands. We have two Canadians imprisoned in China—so much for protecting their human rights. The Chinese government has advised its citizens to avoid Canada. The former premier of Saskatchewan Roy Romanow has called me on a number of occasions to talk of the uneasiness of his province's agricultural producers as the Chinese cease buying their products, just as they did with the midwestern American states in 2018.

What is more, in the Maritimes, where we have thirty-two Liberal MPs in thirty-two ridings, what would happen if China suddenly stopped buying Canadian fish before the election next October? I'm not sure that our government's campaign, imploring other countries to protest, will have much impact on the Asian giant. In any case, many Canadians who do business in China are no longer having their calls returned by their partners and their counterparts. Many no longer travel to China. Universities are nervous, for the presence of Chinese students represents many billions of dollars to our economy, and so on.

In my view, one of the great successes of Pierre Elliott Trudeau in international affairs was to recognize China before the Americans did. As for me, having led two great

Team Canada missions to China, I enjoyed hearing Premier Zhu Rongji say that Canada was China's best friend, because even if I spoke repeatedly about the problem of human rights, we still had very good relations with the second greatest power on the world stage. Today, my country is more unpopular in China than it was under the Harper government and very likely far down on the list of friends of that country, which will one day be the most powerful in the world. I am sad and rather discouraged. Yet I hope I am wrong to be so pessimistic, and I hope Justin is right. Time will tell . . .

Yesterday, March 5, 2019, the Chinese announced that they were suspending purchases from the largest exporter of canola in Canada, Richardson International. Last year, Canada exported $2.5 billion of canola to China, or 50 per cent of Canadian production. Who was it who informed them that the father of our minister of foreign affairs was a producer of canola?

4

THE THREE WISE MEN

During a reception that took place in Ottawa, I'd met Jacques Létourneau of the Confederation of National Trade Unions (CNTU), and we had agreed to get together again, which we did in January 2019 at my Dentons office in Montreal's Place Ville Marie. As we both came from rural backgrounds, he from Thetford Mines and me from Shawinigan, we were soon very much at ease with each other. I told him that one of my first clients in the early days of my career as a lawyer was the Central Council for Mauricie within the Catholic Workers Confederation of Canada (known by the initialism CTCC from its French name), the forerunner of the Confederation of National Trade Unions (the CNTU). After a while, the union leaders with whom I worked told me that their bosses had decided that from then on, all the legal work would be concentrated in a Montreal office.

As I was no longer a lawyer for the unions, I found myself on the opposite side of the table with certain bosses, and when the time came for my election in 1963, I was criticized by the union side for having at times been a lawyer for the bosses. That enabled me to say that if I was perhaps not good enough for them, I was apparently too good to be against them on the other side of the negotiating table. Today's president of the CNTU has informed me that when I was replaced as a lawyer for the Shawinigan Central Council, it was, ironically, Jean Marchand who was the big boss of the CTCC, he who later became a minister in the cabinets of Pearson and Trudeau, and so my colleague for thirteen years. What is more, when I became a federal MP, on a number of occasions the CTCC engaged my services for two arbitrations in the National Capital Region, which pleased me greatly.

On the other hand, when I was a student, I went through a difficult period during the famous Belgo strike, whose union was headed by the renowned Michel Chartrand. Shawinigan was then a very prosperous town thanks to its cheap electricity, and it was the Canadian town with the greatest concentration of factories that relied on electrochemistry. The CNTU controlled all the union sections in each of the factories, which made Shawinigan the most unionized city in Quebec.

Obviously, as the son of a retired machinist, I was very partial to the union movement. The decision to strike at Belgo, a paper mill, was not approved of by many workers, and perhaps 40 per cent of the union members refused to walk out, which enabled the company to partially continue its operations. As my house was very close to the factory, a large number of the Belgo workers lived in our part of town, called La Baie. It was a very hard time in my community. Some heads of families were strikers and others were "scabs," or strike breakers. In certain families, the father was a scab and the son a striker. Sometimes one brother was a scab and the other was on the picket line at the entrance to the factory. Today, still, there are families that never reconciled following this labour conflict.

As the factory was functioning at a slow pace with those workers who had rejected the strike, we were a group of non-union students who had summer jobs, and we had to pass in front of the strikers to go to work. This situation was very embarrassing, because some of the students were the sons of strikers. One afternoon, coming out of the workplace, when tensions were very high on the picket lines, a striker shoved a student, and Michel Chartrand intervened, saying, "Leave him alone. He's a student and not a union member. He'll be gone in a few weeks, that little pr——!" Later, I had the opportunity on many occasions to meet this left-wing radical, the much-loved Chartrand. He could be very good company, for he was pleasant, funny, a good storyteller, a humanist, and very generous.

When I was prime minister, I was given a box of high-grade cigars by the Cuban ambassador to Canada. Because I was not a smoker, I decided to pass them on to a well-known connoisseur: Michel Chartrand. Later, during a television show, Chartrand was asked what was the greatest surprise of his life, and he replied, "To receive a first-class box of cigars from a Liberal prime minister, Jean Chrétien . . ."

As a student leaning politically to the left, I followed with great interest the progress of the 1949 asbestos strike, during the time of Maurice Duplessis. It was a turning point in the political and social life of Quebec. The prime mover of this huge upheaval was Jean Marchand, and among his close collaborators were Pierre Elliott Trudeau and Gérard Pelletier, later my cabinet colleagues for more than thirteen years. During ministerial meetings throughout that time, the past union experiences of Trudeau, Marchand, and Pelletier often came to the surface, and from those I learned a great deal.

Those few years of practice with unions as a young lawyer and my daily contacts later on with the "three wise men" served me well in my positions as minister and as prime minister. When Prime Minister Trudeau named me president of the Treasury Board, responsible for negotiations with federal employees, the day after my swearing in I went to visit the headquarters of the Canadian Labour Congress (CLC), to the surprise of the directors who were in attendance.

After having left my post as prime minister, I was often consulted by politicians, economists, and other experts concerning our success in balancing the national budget in only three years, and in running surpluses over the next seven years of my leadership. Invited one day to a large meeting organized by the *Times of London* and attended by British Prime Minister David Cameron and his chancellor of the exchequer, George Osborne, I was asked how we were able to divest ourselves of 19 per cent of our bureaucrats without having to confront a national strike. I replied that I'd asked the union leaders why they had not walked out in the face of such severe cuts. They replied that they knew I would never change my mind, and I still don't know if that was an insult or a compliment.

I believe that my combined experience with unions as a young lawyer, as a comrade in arms of the Three Wise Men in the cabinet—Marchand, Pelletier, and Trudeau—and as president of the Treasury Board prepared me well for successfully carrying out that operation.

5

THE PILGRIMS SOCIETY

On Thursday, February 28, 2019, I found myself in New York at the request of my colleagues at the law firm Dentons, who had invited me to give an evening talk before the prestigious social club the Pilgrims Society, founded nearly 120 years ago with the aim of encouraging good relations between the United States, Great Britain, and the Commonwealth.

How surprised I was to see that the person who was to introduce me to this distinguished audience was none other than Bill Clinton, who for seven and a half years had been my colleague at the G7 summits, plus those of APEC, NATO, and many others.

His presentation was very complimentary, perhaps even more so than necessary. But what surprised the listeners was his account of our first meeting at the APEC summit in Seattle in November 1993, just a few days after my election as prime minister, when I told him that I ought not to be seen as being too chummy with the U.S. president, as had been the case for my predecessor. Since he'd mentioned that I'd been a useful companion in arms during our years as heads of our respective countries, I recounted in my turn, before this select New York audience, how during the 1995 referendum he had also tried to help me.

Bill Clinton remembered that at a certain juncture, Jacques Chirac, then mayor of Paris and future candidate for the French presidency, had uttered a statement that had made the headlines. This declaration, interpreted as support for the independence cause in Quebec, was predictably repeated over and over by prominent separatists. One Saturday, nine days before the referendum on October 30, 1995, Clinton and I were at the United Nations in New York. At a reception given by Bill and Hillary, Aline and I found ourselves alone with them for a moment, and Bill told me he'd learned of how complicated things seemed to be getting in Quebec. According to him, it would be sad if a country that functioned so well, like Canada, were to find itself in danger of disappearing. Given that, he would be very happy to do something that might help us, if it were possible. I replied that everything had been going well until, twelve days before the referendum date, the Yes forces had in effect removed Quebec Premier Jacques Parizeau as leader of the campaign. His replacement, Lucien Bouchard, had made a huge splash and transformed the twelve-point lead of the No camp into an eight-point disadvantage just nine days before the referendum. After a few minutes of discussion among the four of us, I told him that if he had the opportunity to say what he felt, as Chirac had done, I would be most happy.

In the days that followed, here is what President Clinton declared: "When I was in Canada last year, I said that I thought Canada had served as a model to the United States and to the entire world about how people of different cultures could live together in harmony, respecting their differences, but working together. This vote is a Canadian internal issue for the Canadian people to decide. And I would not presume to interfere with that. I can tell you that a strong and united Canada has been a wonderful partner for the United States and an incredibly important and constructive citizen throughout the entire world."

It goes without saying that the U.S. president's remarks displeased the Yes people even more than those of Chirac did the proponents of the No. The Paris mayor was not in the same league as the president of the United States. It was twenty-four years later, on this evening of February 28, 2019, that I publicly thanked my friend Bill. He was certainly very useful. Canadians owe him a great deal.

Finally, rather than impose a long discourse on those in the audience, I indicated that I'd rather reply to their questions, explaining that in Canada, an exercise to which the prime minister regularly submits himself in the House of Commons is that of responding to the members' questions. In the Parliament of Westminster, the prime minister visits question period only once a week for thirty minutes and requires an advance notice of forty-eight hours regarding the subject to be debated. In Canada, I presented myself in the House three or four times a week for a period of one hour, and I generally replied to half the questions, always with no prior warning. After more than twenty-nine years as minister and prime minister, I'd come to take pleasure in submitting myself to this fundamental exercise in democracy. That was, in fact, the only thing I really missed from politics after my departure.

At the Pilgrims Society that day, for more than an hour, I answered a great variety of questions regarding international politics, free trade, democracy, elections, and racism, always very frankly, injecting an element of humour to help deal with the more controversial subjects.

On free trade, I said that Canada had granted concessions that I might not have agreed to. And to thank Justin Trudeau for having signed, the U.S. president imposed heavy tariffs on softwood lumber, aluminum, and steel. It was even worse where aluminum and steel were concerned, as the United States already showed a surplus vis-à-vis Canada. As for Brexit, I declared that it was a disaster for Britain, and that is what you get when you enter blithely into a referendum, as Prime Minister David Cameron had done. I could have added that General de Gaulle had lost his post as president in the aftermath of an inappropriate referendum held at the wrong time. Where racism was concerned, I affirmed that this sickness, extremely dangerous for democracy, is coming to the fore in several European countries, and that in the

United States it was unnerving to see a former head of the Ku Klux Klan, David Duke, applauding President Trump. I was sure that he would never have applauded Barack Obama. And so why, I asked, do the racists applaud Trump? Because he has a problem!

At the same time as I was addressing this prestigious audience, our prime minister, Justin Trudeau, was being accused of not telling the whole truth about SNC-Lavalin. Therefore, the country was in crisis, the *Globe and Mail* was frankly hysterical, while here, in the United States, the *Washington Post* kept a laconic inventory of President Trump's daily lies. I declared, "In less than thirty months, your president will have lied more than eight hundred times. These eight hundred lies will not have compromised his approval rating by 1 per cent!"

The crowd seemed to appreciate my propensity to say what I thought, and backed up its enthusiasm with warm applause. Among those who approached to thank me, a well-turned-out gentleman came to tell me that he had laughed on hearing me say in jest that Buckingham Palace was a very nice *shack*. He said that when he was visiting the White House, on seeing it, Prince Charles had declared that it was a lovely little house. After our conversation, I asked a former ambassador of my acquaintance who the gentleman was who had just left me. He replied that it was Edward Cox, Richard Nixon's son-in-law, and the chairman of the New York Republican State Committee. I then went back to Ed Cox and apologized for my harsh words directed at the Republican Party president. He kindly replied that he was in overall agreement with me. I have to confess that during my entire presentation, the Democrat Bill Clinton had a smile on his lips.

In any case, I have perhaps inherited the ancestral right to say whatever I think, since my father spent the first ten years of his life in Manchester, New Hampshire, not so far away.

6

PREDICTIONS

About six years ago from the time I write this, in August 2015, more than six weeks before the expected date, Prime Minister Harper paid a visit to the Governor General to ask her to dissolve Parliament and trigger a federal election. Why nearly three months of electoral campaigning rather than the traditional thirty-five days prescribed by law? He was neck and neck with the NDP, led by an experienced politician, Thomas Mulcair, and Justin Trudeau's Liberals trailed in third place. While the media talked about a Harper-Mulcair struggle, the launching of a long election campaign gave time for the young Justin Trudeau to raise his profile. Those forty-one additional days represented for this young man—modern, progressive, athletic, and good-looking—a veritable gift on the part of Harper. Still today, I do not understand why the former prime minister knowingly offered Trudeau forty-one extra days to campaign. Two months before the election, few people foresaw that the Liberals would emerge with a majority government in October 2015.

Obviously, when I ran into people during this campaign, the first question I was asked was "Who's going to win the federal election on October 19?" Many people thought that since I was already active in politics in 1952, president of the Young Liberals at Laval University in 1956, and a federal MP in 1963, I could predict the unpredictable. But I must admit that I've had a hunch about many surprises. For example, during the 1966 provincial election in Quebec, all the observers were convinced that Jean Lesage would easily beat the Union Nationale of Daniel Johnson, who was called "Danny Boy" by the caricaturists of the day. I had seen Johnson at work in the Mauricie valley, finding good candidates and making unpretentious speeches, clear and leavened with a bit of humour.

I went to meet Premier Lesage in La Tuque, in the north of my riding, and drove back with him. On the way, I told him that I feared he might lose the riding of Laviolette. Sure he would win, Lesage replied, "Jean, if we lose Laviolette, it won't be serious, because the way things are going I'll have too many MNAs after the election." A few days later, at the Quebec Liberal caucus in Ottawa, we went around the table, and to everyone's surprise all the rural Quebec MPs said, "Jean Lesage is going to win the election easily, but in my riding, the Liberal candidate seems to be in difficulty." A member passed these views on to Radio-Canada journalist Jean-Marc Poliquin, who reported that the Liberals in Ottawa were no longer certain of Lesage's election. Obviously, the provincial Liberals were incredulous and furious. What was unthinkable at the start of the campaign finally came true on election night, and Daniel Johnson became premier of Quebec.

When the Conservative Party replaced Robert Stanfield in 1976 with a young MP from Alberta, Joe Clark, no one seemed to think, and even less predicted, that he was going to defeat Pierre Trudeau. Everyone made fun of him, tagging him with the nickname "Joe who?" which didn't stop him from becoming prime minister of Canada. In November 1979, Trudeau announced that he was stepping down as leader of the Liberal Party of Canada. Finance Minister John Crosbie jumped at the opportunity to bring in an austerity budget. Surprise, surprise, the budget was defeated in the House of Commons, Prime Minister Joe Clark saw this as a vote of non-confidence in his government, and he called an election for February 1980. Trudeau then withdrew his resignation, reassumed the Liberal leadership, won the election, and formed a majority government. After the election, sitting to the left of Trudeau in Parliament, I showed him a newspaper article noting that of the 106 editorials written during the electoral period, 99 had urged their readers to vote for Joe Clark and the Conservative candidates. Trudeau joked, "Jean, we must have screwed something up—they weren't all against us!"

Speaking of predictions, who would have imagined all that would happen over a period of nine months? As I've participated in federal and provincial elections since 1956, like everyone else I've made predictions about election results, and my colleagues have fed the rumour that I have a special talent for that exercise. It's true that I've surprised them a few times, and here are three examples.

At the start of the October 1995 referendum campaign, the polls gave the No side an advantage of 20 per cent, leading everyone to believe that everything would be easy for them. Seeing that all was going to be lost, the Yes team tried an amazing roll of the dice, and effectively replaced Premier Jacques Parizeau, who was heading the Yes campaign, with Lucien Bouchard, leader of the Bloc Québécois in the federal Parliament. Replacing the leader in the middle of a campaign was something never seen before, and within a few days, the improbable happened: ten days from the vote, the Yes side took a lead of nine points!

There was panic in the No camp. Pierre Trudeau phoned me, very concerned, and I told him that all was not lost, that there were still nine days left in the campaign. I approached Daniel Johnson Jr., leader of the Liberal opposition in Quebec and head of the No team, and together we agreed on a new strategy, according to which we would floor the accelerator at the last minute, just as the Yes camp, confident of its victory on the Friday preceding the vote, was easing up in its efforts.

The night of the referendum, we were all very nervous, and I was at 24 Sussex Drive with Aline, my children, my son-in-law, André Desmarais, and a dozen campaign workers. I knew that the Parti Québécois had never won 50 per cent of the popular vote in an election, and I waited impatiently for the first results, which came from the riding of Îles-de-la-Madeleine, in a different time zone. Since 1952, I've monitored the election results on the Magdalen Islands and instantly seen which way the wind was blowing. The Yes side won with a smaller majority than I anticipated. I then declared to all those around me: "The result will be very close, and the No side will win by 2 per cent of the vote." In fact, it was 1.6 per cent. Was this luck, experience, or both? Who knows?

During my last election, in November 2000, it was Sunday, the day before the vote, and our plane was returning us to Trois-Rivières so I could deliver my last speech of the campaign in Shawinigan. Knowing that this would be the final time that I would be soliciting the support of my voters, the emotion I felt made it hard to begin my speech. Thirty-seven and a half years earlier, I had for the first time asked for the support of these cherished voters of Saint-Maurice, who had chosen me as their MP for twenty-nine years. At one point, I found myself alone with two English-speaking journalists whom I'd known for a long time, and they asked me to share my predictions for the next day's results. I refused to reply, telling them that if I was wrong, they'd make fun of me. They insisted, promising that all would be in confidence if I trusted them. Here is what Roger Smith, one of the two journalists who covered Parliament Hill for CTV for years, wrote on the subject:

On the eve of the 2000 election, Jean Chrétien was confident that his bet to call a hasty election would earn him a sizeable victory and a third consecutive majority.

The prime minister appeared at the campaign wrap party at the Auberge des Gouverneurs in Shawinigan, grabbed a beer and started chatting with reporters. He singled me out.

"Smit," he said with his characteristic pronunciation of my surname. He rarely called me Roger—it was usually Smith. "Smit, tell me what you predict will happen to me tomorrow."

It was a tough question, so I took the time to ponder my response. The polls pointed to a Liberal majority, but there was this niggling suspicion there might be a surprise.

Chrétien had called the election at the end of October, just over three years after the last time the country went to the polls, and some had called the move cynical. Attempts to unite the right had failed, so the conservative opposition remained split between Joe Clark's Progressive Conservatives and the Canadian Alliance, the new incarnation of the Reform Party, whose members had chosen Stockwell Day over Preston Manning as leader in June. The day after his by-election win, Day had shown up to his press conference on a jet-ski, a stunt that drew widespread mockery. Still, many saw him as a younger and more attractive challenger who could cast Chrétien, once again, as "yesterday's man." By calling an early election, Chrétien had calculated that he might catch the new party and its new leader before they could organize and build real momentum.

Chrétien had other reasons to be pro-active. Paul Martin and his supporters were scheming to kick him out of 24 Sussex, and Chrétien knew that if he completed his term, the calls would be louder than ever for him to step aside in favour of his rival. So, with his party doing well in the polls, he called an election and then explained why he thought it was necessary.

"There are two different visions of Canada," he told reporters, "two crystal-clear alternatives."

Some Liberal MPs were concerned that the early vote might not work out for them, as was the case ten years earlier in Ontario when Liberal Premier David Peterson tried a similar tactic. But Chrétien didn't care to listen to the naysayers in his party, even though they had reason to be nervous.

In the leaders' debate, Joe Clark had the upper hand on Chrétien. According to the polls, Chrétien was the most arrogant of the leaders, but also the smartest. Polls put the Liberals in the lead as the campaign ended, the moment when Chrétien put me on the spot.

So what to answer? Parrot the polls or stir him up a bit? I opted for the latter.

"I think you're going to end up with a minority," I told him. "But it will be a strong minority, maybe close to 150 seats."

He burst out laughing. "Smit, you're out to lunch."

"All right, so what's your prediction?" I asked him. He said he wouldn't tell me, because "you guys"—that is, we journalists—would report it. Come on, I insisted, the campaign's over, this party's off the record, you have my word I won't report it. Back and forth we went, until he was convinced of the pledge that my lips were sealed.

"Okay. So, I'm going to tell you: tomorrow, I'm going to win 172 seats."

And the next day, that was exactly the number of seats the Liberals won. A strong majority: 172 seats out of 301, 106 more than the Alliance.

The next day, I reported on CTV how Chrétien hit the nail on the head. At the time, I did not hear from him about it, but years later, reminiscing during a phone call, he reproached me for breaking my promise not to publicly mention his prediction.

"Okay, but the election was over," I told him. "Besides, what are you complaining about? I made you look good, didn't I?"

He couldn't argue. I could imagine him smiling on the other end of the line.

It is August 16, 2019. In a few weeks, Prime Minister Justin Trudeau is going to call an election, and so I'll venture some predictions. I know this is a rash gesture, as I left politics over fifteen years ago. I'm not plugged into the new communications techniques of today's young people, and most of those outside politics whom I consulted have left us. But let's go nevertheless, and if I miss my mark, you can laugh and so will I. The Liberals are going to lose seats in the Maritimes and in the Prairies, and it will be much the same in British Columbia and Ontario. Trudeau will win a few more seats in Quebec. It will be a Liberal government needing the support of a weakened NDP and a stronger Green Party to survive as a minority government. If I'm wrong, it's not serious, because I'm just an old Monday morning quarterback.

7

THE MARTINS

When I became president of the Young Liberals at Laval University in 1956, I met the Honourable Paul Martin Sr., MP from Windsor, Ontario, and a very dynamic minister of health and welfare, at the Reform Club in Quebec City. He made a strong impression on me.

After the Liberals were defeated at the hands of Conservative John Diefenbaker in 1957, the former prime minister and leader of the Liberal Party Louis St. Laurent resigned, and a race for the party leadership began. Clearly, as the former minister of foreign affairs Lester B. Pearson had just received the Nobel Peace Prize for his exceptional work during the Suez crisis, it was certain that if he decided to run for the Liberal leadership, he would be unbeatable. That being said, Paul Martin Sr. had pursued that same ambition for a very long time. And it was perfectly reasonable, because he'd been elected fifteen years before Mike Pearson and had entered the cabinet three years before his eventual opponent. In addition, he had run for the party leadership at the convention that had chosen Louis St. Laurent in 1949, but had withdrawn from the race before the vote.

If Pearson had refused to be a candidate, it's clear that Paul Martin would have become the Liberal Party leader in 1958. But Pearson did enter the race, making Paul Sr.'s task almost impossible. Nonetheless, he decided to accept the challenge.

At the time of the convention, the Liberal delegation from Laval University, which I headed, decided to vote for Pearson, and we arrived in Ottawa wearing Pearson buttons, like the vast majority of the other delegates.

At a certain point, my entire delegation went into the lobby of the Château Laurier hotel, where we encountered Paul Martin Sr., who was holding forth in the middle of the room, vigorously seeking the delegates' support, with limited success. Those from my caucus held a little meeting and agreed that the fate reserved at the convention for the hard work of Paul Martin Sr. was unjust. So we shook his hand, took off our Pearson buttons, and replaced them with those of Martin. Even if we were certain that Pearson's Nobel Prize would get him elected two days later, we were proud of having shifted our allegiance to support that persistent politician who was, unfortunately, the underdog. It marked the beginning of a long friendship with the Windsor MP, who was one of my colleagues in the cabinets of Pearson and Trudeau.

When Prime Minister Pearson resigned in 1968, Paul Martin Sr., then minister of external affairs, announced his candidacy for party leadership. At that point, I had already been minister of state for finance and was then minister of national revenue. I had to inform Paul Sr. that I was obliged to support my mentor, Finance Minister Mitchell Sharp. Suddenly, Pierre Elliott Trudeau entered the race, Trudeaumania exploded, and the fates of Paul Martin and Mitchell Sharp were sealed. Shortly after Trudeau gained power, Martin left public life to become Canada's high commissioner in London. Aline and I visited him and his charming wife, Eleanor, a woman we liked enormously. At the time, he was in his seventies, and he had me sit in an armchair at the Reform Club in London, in front of a huge painting of the great Liberal leader William Ewart Gladstone, elected prime minister of the United Kingdom for the fourth time at the age of eighty-four! I think he still harboured the desire to be prime minister, and I believe he'd have been very good.

When Paul Martin Sr. retired and returned to his beautiful big house in Windsor, every time I travelled to the region as a minister, I made a point of visiting the Martins. I had exceptional political discussions with one of the greatest politicians of his generation, if not the greatest, even if his sense of timing had failed him for each of the five leadership races in which he participated.

When John Turner abandoned the leadership of the party at the June 1990 convention, Paul Jr., Martin's son, became an aspirant in his turn, and therefore my competitor. During the leadership campaign, when I was in Windsor to promote my candidature, I paid a visit, as usual, to the senior Martins. The situation was obviously a bit uncomfortable, and Mrs. Martin confessed to her unease. I told her not to worry, because if her son did not win, he could always take my place when I left ... which is what happened. While I always maintained excellent relations with them, things turned out to be much more complicated with their son, Paul Jr.

I knew Paul Jr. when he was working for Power Corporation in Montreal. He was close to Maurice Strong, the company's president at the time. When Paul Desmarais took over Power, Maurice Strong left the business, and Paul Martin Sr. made him the first president of the Canadian International Development Agency (CIDA). Strong had an exceptional career in the public sector, becoming one of the leading administrators at the United Nations. As for Paul Jr., he continued his career at Power Corporation. As I knew Paul Desmarais well, and his son André became my son-in-law, I met Paul Jr. on many social occasions, and we became friends. As well, many of the Liberal Party social events gave us an opportunity to meet again, politics being our common passion.

In 1986, I left politics to resume my profession as a lawyer, this time in the business world, and my activities brought me frequently to Montreal. One day, Paul Jr. came to see me to discuss politics and to tell me that party leader John Turner had asked him to be in charge of recruiting candidates for forthcoming elections. This meant that he would have to travel across the country. As he was the president and CEO of the Canadian Steamship Lines, I realized at once that he would be using this springboard not so much to help Turner as to prepare to take his place as Opposition leader. He wanted to know, in fact, if, in the event of a future vacancy at the helm of the Liberal Party, I intended to be a candidate. He must have concluded that this would be the case, but it wasn't the answer he was hoping for.

When the leadership race began then, in January 1990, my main rival, as I had foreseen, was Paul Martin Jr. He had spent three years criss-crossing the country to recruit candidates, in theory, for John Turner. In fact, he had set up an impressive network of organizers, taking advantage of his position as a well-known businessman to build up a substantial war chest, to which he himself had generously contributed.

During the previous race for the party leadership, I had run against John Turner and had forced a second vote. As a francophone candidate succeeding another francophone, I was, in theory, handicapped due to the alternation, apparently necessary, between a francophone and an anglophone to head the party. But in 1990, that same presumed principle gave me a head start.

It soon became clear to me that Paul Jr. had worked very hard. This was during the period of constitutional discussions initiated by Prime Minister Brian Mulroney. It was creating a great stir within the country's political class, especially in Quebec, where I was identified with the Trudeau faction, since I had been his minister of justice responsible for the 1980 referendum, the patriation of the Constitution, and the Charter of Rights and Freedoms, all files that were very controversial in Quebec.

During the campaign period from January to June 23, 1990, the Meech Lake accord proposed by Brian Mulroney completely disrupted political debate. As a lawyer, I took a position in support of francophones outside Quebec, who felt threatened by this constitutional proposal. That earned me the wrath of a large part of Quebec's political class. Still, my organization, led by Senator Pietro Rizzuto, obtained the support of the Quebec delegations fairly easily.

During the race for the party leadership, between January and June 1990, the political debate in Canada revolved entirely around Prime Minister Mulroney's constitutional reform package. As I was seen as a disciple of Pierre Trudeau, who was actively opposing the project, it was hard for me to discuss it in Quebec when the delegates and especially the intelligentsia were crying loudly and clearly that the rejection of a distinct society was going to mean the end of Canada. Yet even if this controversy made the front pages in Quebec every day, nothing seemed to harm my campaign there. Martin's organization was having trouble gathering support for an all-candidates debate in that province, and was forced to charter buses and bring in partisans from Toronto so as not to look bad compared to the large numbers loyal to my cause. At one point, the debate became a bit too animated, and Paul's people began hurling insults in my direction, which made my supporters very unhappy. Even worse, the noisiest among them were anglophones from Toronto who massacred the crude words, mastering, it seemed, neither their meaning nor their pronunciation. The impact on my supporters, who made up the bulk of the crowd, was extremely negative.

The campaign for party leader came to an end in Calgary on June 23, 1990, and despite the controversy surrounding the Meech Lake accord, Paul Martin's team's well-filled war chest, and the very determined barricade erected by Bourassa and Peterson, we prevailed on the first round with 57 per cent of the vote to 25 per cent for Martin. The preceding six months had been the most trying time in my political career, but the result was more than satisfying. I went on to embark on a thirteen-and-a-half-year journey as leader of the political party that would know greater success than in almost any Western democracy, the Liberal Party of Canada. To succeed Laurier, Mackenzie King, Pearson, and Trudeau was quite something for "the little guy from Shawinigan"!

During the three years and four months we'd spent in opposition, my relations with Paul had been very good, to the point where I'd asked him to co-chair, along with Chaviva Hošek, the committee to draw up the program I wanted to present to the electorate. The only significant disagreement we had was that Paul wanted me to eliminate, at any cost, the deficit during our first mandate. But I thought that was a promise impossible to keep, because Mulroney's Conservatives had left us a deficit of $42 billion, or 6.2 per cent of the gross national product; a debt that represented more than 67 per cent of the national revenue, with an interest rate of 11 per cent and an unemployment rate of over 11 per cent. And so, instead of promising to balance the budget in five years, I pledged to reduce the deficit to 3 per cent of the gross domestic product, as demanded by the members of the European Economic Community in the context of the Maastricht Treaty. As I like to say, under-promise and over-deliver. That has been the motto of my political career.

When we won the election on October 25, 1993, I had to form a cabinet. What was I going to do with my two main adversaries for the party leadership, Paul Martin and Sheila Copps? It was the strategy of Lincoln, who did not lack for opponents in his own camp when he became president of the United States, that inspired me in forming my cabinet. He had given them the greatest possible responsibilities.

With Copps, it was easy: I named her deputy prime minister and minister of the environment, which delighted her. With Martin, it was much more complicated. I told him that I wanted him to be my finance minister, because I believed that there was no problem more important than the deficit, the national debt, the unemployment rate, and the high interest rates. He replied that that post was the graveyard of politicians, and he wanted to become the new C. D. Howe, the all-powerful minister of industry and commerce under Prime Minister Louis St. Laurent. I retorted that John Turner and I had been finance minister before becoming party leader and prime minister. After a number of exchanges, he told me clearly that he would not accept finance, but that he'd be happy with industry and commerce. Given this refusal, I offered John Manley the post of finance minister, which he accepted. Forty-eight hours before the swearing-in, Martin called me to say that he'd changed his mind and would finally agree to be finance minister. It's clear that had I not insisted, he would never have known all the glory that this post brought him. I had to call John Manley back. He'd been finance minister for only forty-eight hours, but he would have the position again later on.

During the eight and a half years Martin was my finance minister, all went well in general. As I had myself been responsible for this department under Pierre Trudeau, and the government's financial problems were my greatest pre-occupation, this was the minister whose actions I monitored most closely, leading me to intervene perhaps more often than he would have liked. Still, he always said that I'd helped him a lot, and I would add that Michael Wilson, finance minister in the previous government, always claimed that if Brian Mulroney had supported him as I supported Martin, he wouldn't have left the finances in the sorry state in which we found them in 1993. Three years after forming the government, we tabled the first balanced budget in decades.

As of 1999, I began to realize that Paul Martin and his friends were becoming more and more impatient to see me leave. Journalists who seemed partial to Paul's ambitions wrote stories saying I wanted to remain prime minister until the 2000 election in order to satisfy my alleged ambition to be occupying the post at the onset of the new millennium. The Martin clan and his supportive MPs had already begun discussions as to who would be included in the new cabinet. The bilateral meetings between the finance minister and the members were very frequent; and as nothing is really secret on Parliament Hill, I was constantly receiving reports about what was being said among friends during all these activities.

At that time, I had no intention of seeking a third mandate, because I was happy to have won two majority mandates as prime minister and eleven mandates as an MP over a period of thirty-six years—and this without having known a single defeat in the course of that long period of public life. I said to myself, "Why risk it? You never know . . ." What is more, I was convinced that I could have another career outside of politics. I used to say that you don't get rich in politics when the country's prime minister earns less than the worst player in the National Hockey League.

Still, despite my intention not to seek a third mandate, people around me—ministers, MPs, members of my staff, relatives, and friends—told me I should continue to serve, since the country was doing well (unlike in 1993) with a balanced budget, an interest rate one-third of what it was at the beginning of our first mandate, the lowest unemployment rate in twenty years, constitutional peace achieved in the wake of the Clarity Act, a good international profile, and more.

Then everything went south at the biannual Liberal Party convention in Ottawa in February 2000. On the eve of the convention, which took place at the Regal Constellation

Hotel near the Toronto airport, a group of MPs and members of Paul Martin's circle met to prepare a strategy that would force me to do what I intended to do in any case: not seek a third mandate. But such meetings don't remain secret for long. At the opening of the convention, the journalists, having got their hands on the list of participants, scurried after them to ask what they were doing at this meeting. It was embarrassing to hear the preposterous explanations concocted to get out of the bind. Even Paul made headlines by climbing onto an escalator while the journalists were waiting for him at the top. Television cameras filmed the ludicrous spectacle of the finance minister turning around to arduously descend the escalator in the wrong direction. All this controversy was a disaster for the Martin group.

A few of Paul's sympathizers went too far, and Aline, who had been witness to some unseemly behaviour, joined all those who wanted me to go on with my work. And so, bolstered by this support and the blundering of the Martin clan, I announced that I would be extending my political career and seeking a third mandate. I called the election for the autumn of 2000, and obtained my third mandate as prime minister with a majority in the House of Commons larger than the one in the spring of 1997.

Despite the aborted putsch, I kept Paul on as finance minister. He continued his work, and the relations between his office and mine unfolded smoothly. What is more, after having put our public finances in order in 1995, we found ourselves with large surpluses, disbursed as follows: 25 per cent for reducing the debt, 25 per cent for reducing taxes, and 50 per cent primarily for bettering our social programs.

I am happy to say that the impatience of Paul Martin's supporters to have me leave is what persuaded Aline to support my undertaking a third mandate. It was during this last mandate that we introduced a major reform of political party financing, and that we opened the way for the marriage of same sex partners. More important still: it was during that same mandate that we made the decision not to participate in the Iraq war. I do not believe that Paul Martin or Stephen Harper would have said "no" to George W. Bush! After all, the "Martinists" in the caucus supported the Americans' determination to avenge the insult they had received. As for Stephen Harper, he had written in the *Wall Street Journal* that it was a "serious mistake" for Canada not to go to Iraq.

My decision to hold an election in the autumn of 2000 had been a success. The fact that we'd obtained a larger number of seats cooled Martin's ardour, but it was clear that he was very unhappy.

In the spring of 2002, the seventy-five members to whom Paul had promised ministries became somewhat aggressive. Rumours circulated to the effect that Paul was preparing to quit politics. It all came to a head on Friday, May 31, 2002, after a week of skirmishes between my cabinet and Martin's office, with his declaring in Toronto that he was reconsidering his position as finance minister. As of that moment, to my mind, he was no longer minister.

The departure of a finance minister who'd been in that

post for eight years, and in the wake of a controversy, made me fear a major disturbance in the markets on Monday morning. And so the next day, Saturday, I tried to contact Paul by phone. The same thing on Sunday morning, June 2. Only at the end of the morning did he finally take Eddie Goldenberg's call and agree to speak to me around twelve thirty. At my request, Eddie had drafted a very civilized letter of resignation, along with a letter in the same vein accepting it, and he had talked about it to Martin. When Paul phoned me, he was not surprised to learn that his behaviour was unacceptable to me, and that it was up to the prime minister alone to decide who was sitting in the cabinet. That left him the choice of offering his resignation, which would be the most graceful, or being fired. After a long silence, he answered, to my surprise, that he preferred to be fired, which was accomplished immediately. End of conversation.

As I wanted to act rapidly before the markets opened the next morning, I was able to reach John Manley, who was with a cabinet working group at Meech Lake. I told him quite simply that he was the new finance minister, that he had to go home and get a tie, and make his way to the Governor General as soon as possible. At four o'clock, I had a new finance minister, and the press was informed. Paul Martin being expelled from cabinet was big news. All that was left was to await the reaction of the markets the next morning. I was a bit surprised by the markets' reaction to the new finance minister, Manley: only good words and no negative vibrations.

During the previous eight years, Manley had been my minister of industry and commerce and my minister of external affairs. He was intelligent, a hard worker, a man of integrity, a straight talker, and he made the transition seamlessly, he who, eight years earlier, had for two days been finance minister designate when Paul Martin could not decide whether to accept my offer of the job that would make his name. How ironic! It was John Manley who was my last finance minister, and a very fine one.

The excellent book *Team of Rivals*, by the historian Doris Kearns Goodwin, describes the relationship between the American president Abraham Lincoln and his secretary of the treasury Salmon P. Chase. Lincoln was of the opinion that Chase was an excellent treasury secretary, but that he had one problem: presidential fever.

Paul Martin's ambition to prematurely take my place complicated our relations, but not our capacity to work together with our cabinet colleagues to successfully restore our financial health and to promote Canada's economic growth.

8

CLEAR GRIT

This morning, May 11, 2021, I had the pleasure of talking to a retired politician with whom I've always had a friendly and admiring relationship, Robert "Bob" Nixon. When I met Bob Nixon in 1968, he was leader of the opposition in Ontario's legislative assembly. During the race for the leadership of the federal Liberal Party, he supported—as did I—the candidature of the finance minister, Mitchell Sharp, and we were co-presidents of his campaign.

Bob's father, Harry Corwin Nixon, was the provincial member in the region of Brantford for 42 years, until his death in 1961. Harry Nixon was leader of the opposition and briefly the Liberal premier of Ontario in 1943. His son, my friend Bob, succeeded him as a member of the legislature. Bob Nixon was himself leader of the Ontario Liberal Party and leader of the opposition for 10 years over a period of 30 years as a member in his father's electoral riding. Later, Jane Stewart, Bob's daughter, was a candidate on my team during my first election campaign as Liberal leader. She was elected as a federal MP in the same riding her father and grandfather represented at the provincial level for 72 years. Immediately after the 1993 election, Jane Stewart was elected president of the Liberal caucus and became an MP shortly thereafter, one of my best. Along with Sheila Copps, Lucienne Robillard and Ann Maclellan, she was one of the four most impressive women in my cabinet.

When I was a candidate for the Liberal leadership in 1984, I asked Bob Nixon to be the co-president of my campaign. As leader of the Ontario Liberal Party and leader of the opposition, he told me that many militants thought that after Trudeau they had to select an anglophone leader, but in his opinion what was most important was to vote for the best candidate, whatever the native tongue. And he thought that I was the one who ought to be chosen by the convention. He warned me that the notion of alternation would make for a hard race, but he was going to do his level best to help me.

He decided to hold a public meeting at his family farm, and we addressed some hundreds of supporters from the balcony of the ancestral mansion built in 1853. During his presentation, talking about his candidate Jean Chrétien, he declared, among other things, that the liberals in his region could count on me because I was a "clear grit." This declaration triggered a burst of applause. As for me, I had not quite grasped the meaning of the two words. When I left the meeting for another event, I had as a driver a retired gentleman who was a long-time Liberal supporter. I took the opportunity to ask him what Nixon meant to say in describing me as a "clear grit." He began to explain to me, with some emotion, why he himself was a "clear grit." He said that when his grandfather was on his deathbed, he brought together all his children and asked them to swear that none of them, ever, nor their children, nor their descendants, would vote for the Conservative Party, and all promised to respect his wishes. When I asked him why his grandfather had acted in such a way, he replied that it was because he was a clear grit—in other words a descendant of those Scottish immigrants who, during a difficult period in the second half of the 19th century, had lost their lands to the Conservative bankers of Kingston, known as the Family Compact. The descendants of those Scottish immigrants felt that the only way to get even for the hard times they then endured was never to vote for the Conservatives, who for them embodied the political party of those corrupt Family Compact bankers. And so Bob Nixon told the Liberal supporters that I was not in the bankers' pocket, that I was born in rural Quebec, and that I was to his mind the best candidate for the Liberal Party leadership. Thanks to that intervention of the Ontario legislature's opposition leader, we did better than expected among the delegates of that region.

After 10 years as leader of the Ontario Liberal Party, Bob Nixon gave way to David Peterson, who became premier of Ontario in 1985. Bob became his finance minister. Later, during the race for the leadership of the federal Liberal Party in 1990, a situation developed that perhaps led, without my knowing it, to my depriving my friend Bob Nixon of the opportunity to become premier of Ontario, following in the footsteps of his father Harry in 1943.

Several months after I was elected leader of the Liberal Party of Canada, I learned that David Peterson had already decided to run for the leadership of the party when I'd met him in Toronto after my encounter in Quebec with Robert Bourassa. In fact, he'd discussed with his finance minister, Bob Nixon, the possibility of a transition of power favoring his best known and most prestigious minister. I don't know if my confrontation with Peterson and Bourassa played a significant role in the Ontario premier's withdrawal from the race. Personally, I believe that it did, and that unintentionally I compromised my friend Bob Nixon's chance to become premier of his province, like his father in 1943. I'm sure that he would have been a very good government leader.

I wanted to write about the Nixon family because I see there a beautiful story of a commitment to public life. One hundred and one years ago, Harry Nixon became a provincial member of the legislature. From 1919 to 1961 he served as a member, as leader of the Ontario Liberal Party, leader of the opposition, and premier of the most populous province in the country. In 1961 his son Bob replaced him, and for 30 years, until 1991, he was the provincial member for this semi-rural, semi-urban riding. As well as being a member like his father, he was leader of the Ontario Liberal Party and leader of the opposition for 10 years. When he left politics, he continued his public service as Ontario's delegate to London, and then as chairman of the board for Atomic Energy of Canada Limited. In 1993, Robert Nixon's daughter, Jane Stewart, was elected as a member of parliament in the same federal riding, and was a very competent minister, much respected by her colleagues, the press, and the bureaucracy, as well as being a delightful companion for all who knew her. When she left the Canadian parliament, she was recruited by the United Nations and continued to serve in the public sector in New York and Geneva.

What is remarkable about the Nixon family—Harry, Robert, and Jane—is that after distinguished careers in public life, they all continued to reside in their region. One after the other, each of them occupied the house known as "Woodview," built in 1853 on the land of the family farm. Unlike so many others who retired to the big city of Toronto and became members of the provincial capital's upper class, all three went back to live among those who had elected them.

I salute three generations of Nixons, who served Ontario and Canada with conviction, honour, and dignity, from 1917 to 2017, from Harry's first election to Jane's retirement from the United Nations.

9

JUSTICE AND THE DEATH PENALTY

One day in Shawinigan, I met a member of a family with whom I was acquainted, and found myself swept back into problems that were part and parcel of my daily life when I was a novice lawyer, exactly sixty years ago. He began talking to me about his grandson's problems with the police. The poor young man was getting into trouble because he was not receiving the treatments he needed for his mental illness. His lawyer spent hours dealing with his situation without receiving any financial compensation because, despite his setbacks, the young man was very likeable.

All this took me back to the period between 1959 and 1964, when I was earning my living as a lawyer in a small town. To make ends meet, you couldn't be too picky: one day it was civil law, the next commercial law, and then family or criminal law. And sometimes, you even became a family's social worker, as was the case with my friend's grandson.

But looking back, those youthful years practising law

JEAN CHRÉTIEN

have left me with some very pleasant memories. The range of cases I was involved with was unbelievable, compared to the work lawyers do today in the large national and international offices I frequent. One specialist for this, another for that, and so on. We, the young lawyers called to the bar in Trois-Rivières, had to specialize in everything and make do all the time.

In those days, there was no law court in Shawinigan, but every Friday a judge with the Court of Sessions of the Peace visited a police station courtroom to hear cases involving small and middling violations. As I went there every Friday, I accepted those cases of little importance, such as speeding, illegal parking, and other minor infractions. For small sins of this type, we could submit confessions in the absence of the accused. That showed the public, always present in good numbers, that I was very much in demand, and this gave me some publicity. Therefore, my Fridays were very full, and it all led to my pleading more serious cases. As criminal law was only heard one day a week, I spent all day at court, where the hearings were often very animated.

Because I was extremely busy one day a week with criminal law, and always as a defender, one of my electoral opponents accused me of being a lawyer for organized crime, as if the underworld was active in this small town. On a number of occasions, I defended a well-known local criminal named Bundock, and I had to defend myself as well for being this notorious individual's lawyer, not denying the fact, but asserting that I was doing it at the request

61

of his father, someone much appreciated in the region. I added that it was my professional duty to do it, and addressing my voters via television, I said, "If one of you had a son who was in trouble with the law, you'd be very glad to find a competent lawyer to defend him. That's what I'm doing." That ended the controversy.

Devoting, in those days, almost 20 per cent of my time to criminal law, I found the work very interesting and rewarding, because it introduced me to some of the most unusual people in society. There was a client called Monsieur C., whom the police knew only too well. In fact, every time someone was up to no good, C. was instantly suspected, sometimes wrongfully. One day, after being charged with theft and assault with violence, he came to tell me that he had not committed the crime, therefore he was innocent, and that he had an alibi. So I said to him, "If you have an alibi, you'll be acquitted." He replied, "Well, I was in a motel with my brother's wife at the time of the crime, and I don't want to use this alibi because, what with my other convictions, I've already humiliated my family enough."

As he was on the police list of those always presumed to be guilty, a case was built against him. C. had no other defence than to swear that he was innocent. The judge preferred to believe the police, and he was sentenced to prison. Even though he had on certain occasions committed reprehensible acts, he harboured in the depths of his soul a certain sense of dignity that deterred him from further humiliating his brother and the rest of his family, even if he had to go to jail. I've ever since retained a vivid memory of this young man, whose faults, however many there were, had not deprived him of a deep sense of honour.

As I like to make people smile, it's in that spirit that I'm going to unearth this next memory. Madame B. was well known as a practitioner of the world's oldest profession. One day, the police arrested her and charged her with prostitution. I told her that she had no other choice than to plead guilty, but I would try to persuade the judge that she should receive as lenient a penalty as possible. This was at a time when the town of Shawinigan was the site of many strikes. The judge was known to be socially conservative and had been appointed by Maurice Duplessis. And so, even if at the time I was intervening on a regular basis in defence of unionized workers, I decided to flatter the judge by appealing to his social convictions. I told him that this poor Madame B. was the product of an unstable climate that flourished in the town because of the unions, which were fomenting all this chaos with their strikes, etc. The judge took pity on her and imposed a ten-dollar fine, advising her not to fall into sin!

Leaving the court, she drew herself up to her full five feet and called out to the police, taunting them, "So you three big lunks came to arrest me, and it only cost me ten dollars. Ha, ha, ha!" The police, furious, decided to lay a trap for her.

They hired a man to solicit Madame B. in a bar in order to be able to arrest her again, drag her into court, and punish her for her insolence.

During the trial, everyone was surprised to see that we were actually presenting a defence. The hireling testified that he had solicited Madame B., that he'd given her money, and that they had then retired to Room 32. In my cross-examination, I made him admit that once they were in the room, there was no sexual contact, and that's how the encounter ended. When I questioned the policeman responsible for the case, who was also the chief of police, a tall, attractive man who was proud and very sure of himself, I reminded him that there was no sexual activity and so no prostitution. I added that he ought not to be using taxpayers' money to try to lure a poor, single mother into vice, and laughter rose up from the curious citizens filling the courtroom during this Friday afternoon session. The judge, from behind the bench, pronounced a verdict of not guilty. The police chief left the courtroom, enraged, and I'd be surprised if he ever voted for me thereafter.

When you're a young twenty-six-year-old lawyer and you find yourself with a client who has just been arrested by the police and is accused of murder, I can attest that it gives you plenty of butterflies in your stomach. One day, the mother of a young man my age, and whom I knew, phoned me in tears to tell me that her son Jules was being charged with murder and was locked up in Trois-Rivières. She asked if I would be his lawyer. As it was a family that lived in the neighbourhood where I was born, I took the case, but with great apprehension, as the death penalty was still in force. And I knew there was going to be a lot of talk, because murders in the region were very rare. As the event had taken place at the Château de Blois in Trois-Rivières, I asked my university friend Pierre Garceau to help me, because he practised law in the neighbouring town of Laviolette.

The accused, Huard, had been drunk in a bar when a prostitute offered him her services, which he accepted. They went up to a room together. An argument broke out, Huard lost his cool, and strangled the sex worker. The police had no trouble locating the accused. They arrested him, threw him in prison, and charged him with murder. The situation was clear: the accused was facing the death penalty, and I was his lawyer. What to do?

Pierre and I went to see Huard to ask him about the crime. He confirmed that he'd been drinking, but he was not usually a drinker. He also told us that he was hotheaded, and once they were in the room and engaged in intense sexual activity, the young woman suddenly stopped to ask him for more money. This demand put him in a rage and plunged him into an abyss. When he came to his senses, he realized that he'd strangled the poor woman. His account did not give us much wiggle room for building a plausible defence.

In 1960, there wasn't as much news as there is today, and so the Huard trial made the headlines, and our colleagues wondered what sort of defence we were going to present.

As defence lawyers, it was our duty to do everything possible to save our client from the gallows. And so we pled "provocation," hoping to avoid a verdict of premeditation. To do so, we had to know more about the unfortunate victim, a woman well known in the community.

And so we summoned to the witness box a certain Claude, a local figure who was familiar to all and very funny. Suddenly the atmosphere shifted from the tragic to the comic. This witness knew the poor victim well, and was privy to her not very orthodox behaviour. Dear Monsieur Claude was the most useful witness I ever met.

It all ended with a verdict of involuntary homicide, and our client was condemned to five years in prison. As for Pierre Garceau and me, we had realized the dream of any young lawyer: we'd saved an accused from the gallows.

Sixteen years later, on July 14, 1976, as an MP, I voted for the abolition of the death penalty, which put an end to hanging in Canada.

10

FRIENDSHIP VERSUS POLITICS

I n September 1955, at the age of twenty-one, I entered the
law faculty at Laval University in Quebec City. The change
this made in my student life, and my life as a young man, was
unbelievable. I had just spent thirteen of the last fifteen years
under constant surveillance in boarding schools, and suddenly
I found myself with no disciplinary overseer, no monitor in
the study halls and the playgrounds (which were, in any case,
surrounded by high fences)—what freedom!

The faculty of law provided a natural forum for political
discussions between students who would be future lawyers
or notaries. These discussions were frequent and very lively,
because Laval University was located in the heart of Quebec
City, and its law faculty was situated very near the provincial
legislature. The premier at the time was the famous and very
controversial Maurice Duplessis. Our professors did not
teach full-time, as they had careers as lawyers and practising
notaries, so our courses were given in the morning from

8:00 to 10:00, and in the afternoon from 4:00 to 6:00. Outside these hours, we roamed freely through the magnificent ancient streets of old Quebec. What happiness!

During this free time, the students from Quebec City generally went home. Those who came from elsewhere, like me, usually lived in small boarding-house rooms, and since we had about six hours to study or to kill time, we gathered in the student centre or the tavern, Chez Bourgault, near the law faculty, to hold animated discussions concerning politics or sports. We were, for the most part, salon revolutionaries, opposed to the very conservative governments of Duplessis provincially and of John Diefenbaker federally.

Among our chattering gang was an amusing little guy, well informed, talkative, and determined, who faced off with us. His name was Roméo Roy, and he'd done his *cours classique* first at Sainte-Anne-de-la-Pocatière, and then at the Trois-Rivières seminary for two years, before finishing his studies and obtaining his B.A., and then embarking on his law studies. I'd known him at Trois-Rivières, and we were good friends, even if in our political discussions during leisure hours Roméo was a fervent defender of Duplessis's and Diefenbaker's politics, in contrast to most of the other students, who took part in every demonstration against Duplessis. During our six years of schooling together, Roméo and I disagreed on politics while remaining good friends.

Once he became a notary, Roméo opened his office in the small town of Sainte-Anne-de-la-Pocatière, where he practised his profession with success until his retirement. As for me, at the age of twenty-nine, after a few years practising law in Shawinigan, I began my long career in federal politics, which lasted forty years. From the Duplessiste he had been at college and university, Roméo drifted toward the Parti Québécois of René Lévesque, whose cause he embraced with admirable fervour. Politically, I was at the other extreme. As a Liberal at the federal level, I became a minister under Lester B. Pearson and Pierre Trudeau, and later prime minister of Canada. As much as I was for the No side in the two referendums on Quebec separation, Roméo was for the Yes.

Several times during my long career, I had to visit Sainte-Anne-de-la-Pocatière to make a speech in support of Liberal candidates. Before going to the political meeting, I always stopped by to see Roméo, to greet him and his charming wife, Brigitte. I invited him to come and hear my talk before the Liberal supporters, but each time he refused, saying that it would be sacrilege for the separatist Roméo Roy to attend a speech given by the "cursed" federalist Chrétien. His political convictions prevented him from making a gesture that would contradict his nationalist thinking, but we remained good friends.

When I became prime minister of Canada, I invited all my fellow classmates from the law faculty to a reception at 24 Sussex Drive. And I was very surprised when I saw Roméo and Brigitte arrive. Aline and I were delighted to be able to welcome them. Roméo admitted that he would never have thought that he would one day find himself in Ontario at the residence of Canada's prime minister, the home of a

Quebec federalist and a Liberal to boot—he who had never voted Liberal in his life, even if his old friend Jean Chrétien was leader of the party. Either we have convictions or we don't!

In October 2009, I was retired, and Jean de Brabant, the son of my friend Michelle Tisseyre, the well-known television host who had campaigned along with me for the No side during the 1980 referendum, sent me his book, *Comment tripler sa mémoire après 50 ans* (*How to Triple Your Memory after 50*), and asked if I would write a short prologue for the second edition. In what I wrote, I concluded that I ought to follow the author's advice, because if we don't exercise our memory, it disappears.

So at the age of seventy-five, I began to memorize poetry. I talked to my friend Roméo, who had been the star of our class when it came to reciting poems, and he began to give me suggestions. Every time we had a telephone conversation, he asked me to recite the last poem I had memorized. Thanks to Jean de Brabant and Roméo Roy, I memorized more than fifty poems by the great names of French and French-Canadian literature: Paul Verlaine, Victor Hugo, Paul Éluard, Charles Baudelaire, Émile Nelligan, Guillaume Apollinaire, Sully Prudhomme, Anne Hébert, Edmond Rostand, a dozen La Fontaine fables, and a number of others. I spent many delightful hours in the presence of these cultural treasures, and I was, at the same time, sharpening my memory! Along the way, my desire to pick up my pen and write *My Stories, My Times* grew apace. It was published when I was eighty-four, and I have kept on going, thanks to a memory still in working order in 2019.

My classmates from the Collège de Trois-Rivières have for more than sixty years had the excellent idea of getting together annually, and whenever I can, I join them. A few years ago, our president, Marcel Beauchemin, called me to say that Roméo Roy had contacted him to ask if I was going to be present. If so, he asked permission to say a few words. He said he was afraid that Roméo might reproach me for my political convictions. I replied that he had to let Roméo speak, and that if he attacked me, we would be treated to a good open debate.

When we all arrived at the college a few weeks later, Beauchemin gave the floor to our dear Roméo. Instead of laying into me, he dedicated a poem to me, which he recited by heart: "Le sommeil du condor" by Charles-Marie-René Leconte de Lisle, a superb allegory about a majestic bird that rises so high over the Andes mountain range that it can see the Atlantic Ocean on one side and the Pacific on the other. That was Roméo's way of paying homage to me for my ten years as leader of the country. Coming from a devout separatist, it was extremely moving.

Later, along with Aline, I went to visit Roméo and Brigitte in their lovely house on Sainte-Anne-de-la-Pocatière's main street. After lunch, Roméo had me visit his college, which he had long ago been forced to leave, with the result that he became my fellow student at Trois-Rivières. When we arrived on the site, we met at least fifty students who were there to take a French course during their summer vacation. These anglophone students came from all the Canadian provinces, from Newfoundland to British Columbia. They were very surprised and happy to meet a former prime minister whom they'd known from the daily papers only a few years earlier. For twenty minutes, we had a good time talking together. I then suggested that they come to Roméo's office to talk some more, by necessity in French, because Roméo was not really bilingual. I told them that what would be most interesting for them, as English Canadians, would be to have a respectful discussion with a true hardline separatist, because Roméo was more French than the French in the Old World.

In 2015, Brigitte, Roméo's wife, called to tell me that her husband was in palliative care at the hospital in Sainte-Anne-de-la-Pocatière. Aline and I went to say goodbye. On his death bed, he asked me to recite two of the most beautiful poems in French literature, "Demain dès l'aube" by Victor Hugo and "Le vase brisé" by Sully Prudhomme. That was our last meeting.

Politics is one thing; friendship is another. And despite their differences, I have always thought that the two ought not necessarily be incompatible.

Demain, dès l'aube

Demain, dès l'aube, à l'heure où blanchit la campagne,
Je partirai. Vois-tu, je sais que tu m'attends.
J'irai par la forêt, j'irai par la montagne.
Je ne puis demeurer loin de toi plus longtemps.

Je marcherai les yeux fixés sur mes pensées,
Sans rien voir au dehors, sans entendre aucun bruit,
Seul, inconnu, le dos courbé, les mains croisées,
Triste, et le jour pour moi sera comme la nuit.

Je ne regarderai ni l'or du soir qui tombe,
Ni les voiles au loin descendant vers Honfleur,
Et, quand j'arriverai, je mettrai sur ta tombe
Un bouquet de houx vert et de bruyère en fleur.

Tomorrow, At Dawn

Tomorrow at dawn, when the fields go pale,
I will leave. You are awaiting me, I know.
I will go by the woods, I will go by the hills,
I can no longer be far-off from you.

I will walk, eyes bent on my thoughts,
Blind to the beyond, deaf to all sound,
Alone, unknown, back bent, hands crossed,
Saddened, where day is as night.

I will not see the evening's declining gold,
Nor the distant sails, Honfleur bound,
And when I arrive, set down on your tomb
A bouquet of green holly and heather in bloom.

11

THE FIFTIETH ANNIVERSARY OF VE DAY

June 2019. A few days ago, on the Normandy coast, there were large demonstrations to mark the seventy-fifth anniversary of the Normandy landing, in which chiefs of state and government leaders participated. Among these were Prime Minister Justin Trudeau, U.S. President Donald Trump, German Chancellor Angela Merkel, and French President Emmanuel Macron. I had been in the same position on the fiftieth anniversary of the victory, which was celebrated with great pomp, and I am reminded of some anecdotes I'd like to share twenty-five years on.

It all began in Buckingham Palace in London, where Queen Elizabeth and Prince Philip were receiving the heads of state and government leaders, as well as other guests, in the great halls, elegant and historic, of this immense castle. Following tradition, the women were all dressed very elegantly and wore large hats. Aline and I were talking with

James Bolger, prime minister of New Zealand, and his wife, when a major-domo approached to inform me that the Queen wanted to see me in her office. I went straight there, wondering why the sovereign wanted to talk with me. In fact, she wished to consult me regarding a delicate situation she had to manage involving my friend the prime minister of New Zealand.

James Bolger had asked the Queen to visit his country and to apologize, in the name of the British monarchy, for the historic fate reserved for the indigenous Maoris under the colonial British administration. She seemed very put out and feared creating an untenable precedent, all the more so in that Bolger was one of the leaders of the movement seeking to abolish the monarchy in his country. I saw immediately that if the Queen accepted my friend's request, she would place herself in a most uncomfortable position, given that the Commonwealth has fifty-four member states, many of which could very well make similar demands.

To lighten the mood a bit, I told her, jokingly, "Your Majesty, if you make a beginning, I will be forced to have you come to Canada. And as we have several hundred Indigenous communities, you will be on your knees for at least two years. And what about the situation you will face in India?" Eventually, I returned to Aline, who was looking for me, as her large hat had prevented her from seeing me leave. Bolger was still with her, and I put my hand on his shoulder and began to talk to him about my meeting with the Queen. Her Majesty suddenly came our way, without saying a word, and gave me a wink of approval, to the surprise and astonishment of Aline and her two companions. Of course, the Queen never visited the magnificent country of New Zealand to apologize. In time, if there were regrets expressed, they came from national governments.

That same evening, the heads of state and government leaders present were invited to spend the night on the royal yacht *Britannia*. After an elegant cocktail party in the magnificent vessel's grand salons, we were seated with Queen Elizabeth and Prince Philip. I was installed to the Queen's left, and to her right was Lech Walesa, the celebrated Dansk electrician who became president of Poland in the wake of the Soviet Union's collapse. The sovereign talked to me in French, and a translator was needed for the Polish president, who spoke only his native tongue.

Suddenly, President Walesa addressed himself to me, asking why we wanted to abolish the monarchy in Canada. A very delicate question when you're seated next to the Queen herself, very attentive, of course, to our conversation, with a little smile at the corner of her mouth. I replied that the abolition of the monarchy was not a political issue in Canada. The Queen then spoke to Bolger, who was sitting on the other side of Walesa, to ask him why he wanted to abolish the monarchy in New Zealand when it was not a preoccupation for Chrétien in Canada. That was a difficult moment for poor Bolger!

After the meal, I found myself with Bolger and Paul Keating, the prime minister of Australia. Bolger told Keating that I had placed him in an embarrassing situation in declaring that the abolition of the monarchy was not an urgent matter in Canada. So I said to my colleagues that I had enough problems with the separatists in Quebec and didn't need any more with the loyalists in Ontario and British Columbia, putting emphasis on the word *British*. Keating had been an abolitionist when his country was rife with debate on the subject, to the point of holding a national referendum on the subject. So he remarked to me, with his very Australian accent, "Don't worry, Jean, we'll blaze the trail for you."

In fact, when a referendum was held during the administration of his successor, John Howard, the proposition concerning the abolition of the monarchy was defeated. Prime Minister Howard, a fervent monarchist, won his gamble with a three-part question, which needed at least 50 per cent of the vote to pass. As none of the three propositions obtained the support required, the monarchy still exists in that beautiful Southern Ocean country. Very shrewd, our dear John!

After a restful night on board the famous *Britannia*, we shared a breakfast with neighbours in the next room: Václav Havel and his wife. He was a writer, a revolutionary, a fascinating character, and the first elected president of the Czech Republic. We then docked in France before a large crowd that awaited the Queen and twenty heads of state and government leaders.

We had arrived on the Normandy beaches, where French President François Mitterrand awaited us with fifty more

There are three Canadian prime ministers in this photograph.
Who is the third?

The famous "Thibaudeau moose."

I preferred meetings that were relaxed, and I enjoyed making my companions laugh—here, John Turner and Pierre Elliott Trudeau.

Jiang Zemin, president of China.

I made the famous golfer Fred Couples laugh heartily.

Queen Beatrix of the Netherlands.

Two Conservative prime ministers and two Liberal prime ministers:
Kim Campbell, Joe Clark, Pierre Elliott Trudeau and myself.

Stephen Harper: you see, he could smile!

Ryutaro Hashimoto, prime minister of Japan.

Gerhard Schröder, chancellor of Germany.

Zhu Rongji, premier of China, and André Desmarais, my son-in-law, near my dear Aline with her smiling eyes.

Ernesto Zedillo, president of Mexico, and his wife, Nilda Patricia Velasco.

Daniel Johnson and Jean Charest, all smiles.

With the voters in a restaurant in Shawinigan.

Yasser Arafat, president of the Palestine Liberation Organization, and his wife, Suha.

George W. Bush, president of the United States, and I had a warm relationship.

Even Fidel Castro liked a good laugh.

With my friend Bill Clinton.

A welcoming crowd during a trip to China.

I have sometimes, on important occasions, climbed onto a desk to talk to my caucus.

In the House of Commons during question period.

There was at least one person listening to me that day . . .

In Moscow's magnificent Red Square.

I liked keeping journalists on the run.

I have never renounced my origins: I was born in rural Quebec, and I'm always at ease with the farmers.

Prince Rainier III of Monaco and my wife.

On an official visit to Cotonou, Benin.

I loved meeting the voters during an electoral campaign.

The night when I became the prime minister of Canada, in October 1993.

Judge Beverley McLachlin being sworn in as chief justice of the
Supreme Court. With Mel Cappe, clerk of the Privy Council
and Governor General Adrienne Clarkson on the left, and the
Governor General's aide-de-camp, Jocelyn Turgeon on the right.

Don Macdonald: he would have been an excellent prime minister.

John Major and I, in front of 10 Downing Street.

Ryutaro Hashimoto, prime minister of Japan, thought that I was tired.

government leaders to pay homage to those who had sacrificed their lives for our freedom. It was a beautiful ceremony as only the French know how to organize: impeccable in its dignity, order, colour, and deep feeling.

I then moved on to Juno Beach, at Courseulles-sur-Mer, where the Canadian soldiers had disembarked at the time, and I inaugurated a beautiful pavilion that recounts the historical achievements of our young compatriots. The French government was represented by the justice minister, Simone Veil, who had survived internment in the abominable concentration camp of Auschwitz. I had carefully prepared the speech I was to deliver before the hundreds of veterans and French citizens. I invoked the name of the chief of the Indian band to which my diplomatic adviser, James Bartleman, belonged, and who died in Normandy, as well as the names of my brother-in-law Jacques Suzor's five friends, who perished during the Italian campaign. Jacques was the only one who survived out of a group of six Shawinigan friends who signed up to serve in a tank division of the Canadian Army in Europe.

As we were going to visit the cemetery where hundreds of young Canadians lie, I said that in death, those laid to rest in this place were neither French, nor British, nor Polish, nor Ukrainian; in death, they were neither Protestant, nor Catholic, nor Jewish, nor Muslim; in death, they were all Canadian heroes whom we could not forget. It was one of the great moments of my career in public life. Then I took my seat once more beside that great lady Simone Veil, certainly the most respected politician in France, who could not hold back her tears, thinking of those months of horror spent in Auschwitz, and those young people in their twenties and sometimes younger who gave their lives for its liberation and freedom for us all. In paying tribute to them, I too had to contain my emotions. What a memorable day!

We then proceeded to the Netherlands, where we were welcomed by thousands of Dutch waving Canadian flags in tribute to the Canadian soldiers who liberated their country. The country has not forgotten, and every year it sends 20,000 of tulips to our national capital. That is the origin of our famous Tulip Festival, which takes place in Ottawa every May.

On the first morning, Aline and I met the Dutch queen for coffee. She was alone and served us herself. Obviously, our conversation was very agreeable, because my visit was associated with the memory of the Canadian soldiers who had freed her country from the Nazi yoke. In exile, the Dutch royal family took refuge in Canada, where they occupied for several years a beautiful house on Acacia Avenue. The queen has excellent memories of our country, which was a welcoming land for her and the birthplace of her sister Margriet in 1943.

This residence on Acacia Avenue now bears the name of Stornoway, and Aline and I occupied it when I was leader of the Opposition. That house became the property of the Conservative Party when George Drew, on agreeing to leave his post as premier of Ontario to lead the Progressive Conservatives as leader of the Opposition in Ottawa, demanded that the party buy an official house in the national capital. Some time later, the leaders of the Progressive Conservative Party, in financial difficulty, asked the Liberal Party to help them out of a tough spot. That is how Stornoway became the property of the state and the official residence of the leader of the Opposition. It's my belief that we are probably the only country in the world that treats the chief of the Opposition so well.

After our visit to the Royal Palace, we moved on to a military cemetery, where hundreds of young Canadians lie. Before the ceremony began, as we were waiting for Princess Margriet, my friend Lawrence MacAulay, minister of veterans affairs, offered Aline a coffee. Everyone knows the legendary humility of my wife, but to make us smile, she said to Lawrence, "No, thank you, Minister. I've just had one with the Dutch queen, and I'm going to have the next one at Buckingham Palace this evening with Queen Elizabeth." Indeed, we found ourselves once more in London at the end of the afternoon, and dined, along with other guests, with the Queen and Prince Philip. When coffee hour arrived, I told Aline that there were not many girls from rural Quebec who could say that they had drunk coffee with the queen of the Netherlands in the morning, and the Queen of England in the evening.

At noon, the country's political leaders hosted a great banquet to bring to a close our official visit to their country. Our delegation, which included many veterans who fought for freedom, joined the hall full of dignitaries. As is always the case in the old countries, the tables and decorations were of great elegance, with a profusion of Canadian and Dutch flags. The Dutch prime minister and the mayor of Amsterdam made moving speeches. We could not have ended our visit in a more agreeable way.

This fiftieth anniversary of the victory in Europe was also the occasion for celebrations in Russia, which impressed me enormously as well. In May 2015, the Russians celebrated the seventieth anniversary of the victory over Nazi Germany, but their Western allies boycotted the Moscow ceremony. I found that deplorable, because it must be acknowledged that if Adolf Hitler had not attacked Russia in 1941, breaking their non-aggression pact, it is probable that we would have lost the war to Germany. What is more, it's worth remembering that it was the Russians, not the Americans, who first entered Berlin. And so I found the military parade on Red Square to commemorate the fiftieth anniversary of the victory truly overwhelming. The emotion was palpable in the crowd when thousands of veterans, draped in medals and proud to display them, filed by us, hundreds of them in wheelchairs or supported on crutches, war amputees much weakened after more than fifty years.

The most difficult moment was when Boris Yeltsin's wife, who had lost all her family during the war, collapsed in sorrow into Aline's arms. We often forget that the Russians are those who suffered the most among the Allies, with more than 20 million dead. There was no viable reason for us in the West to boycott a tribute whose purpose was to honour those valiant fighters who did more than their share to ensure a victory whose blessings we all share. Just imagine for a moment what the world would be like today if Hitler had triumphed.

12

MENG WANZHOU AGAIN

It's July 4, 2019, and today I am turning again to the
Meng Wanzhou saga, which has continued to make
headlines since I wrote about it last winter. Clearly, the dis-
pleasure of the Chinese government has not lessened—on
the contrary—and Canada is paying an ever-greater price.
After the boycott of oil and canola, there came that of peas,
soya, and pork. Businesspeople are complaining that their
Chinese partners are not returning their calls. It's hard to
measure the consequences of this diplomatic imbroglio with
the second largest economy in the world, but the long- and
short-term consequences are very serious.

I have to admit that since the beginning of December
2018, I've been having discussions of varying intensity with
our government. As well, I've received many calls from
businesspeople, politicians, and citizens concerned about
this situation. I have participated in group discussions on a
number of occasions, and I have refused to grant interviews

to the press so as not to cause difficulties for the government. But now, former prime minister Brian Mulroney has suggested publicly on three occasions that Trudeau should ask Jean Chrétien to take the dossier in hand. Such a recommendation, coming from one of my fiercest political opponents, surprised me greatly. But very well, here I am publicly implicated in the dossier, which complicates my life, because I am still talking a little with the prime minister, Minister of Foreign Affairs Chrystia Freeland, and Minister of International Trade Jim Carr.

I understand the prime minister's dilemma, because he is caught between my opinion and that of Ms. Freeland and a small majority of her other advisers. Now, the view of his minister of foreign affairs is utterly incompatible with mine. The minister says that Canada must hew to the law, let the courts decide on the extradition of our Chinese prisoner, and demand that the Chinese free the two Canadians imprisoned after being accused of espionage. And to free them, it is suggested that we ask our allies to apply pressure on Beijing.

We must acknowledge that there have been declarations of support from certain governments over recent months, but with no apparent result. Trudeau went to Washington to beg President Trump to raise the problem with Chinese President Xi Jinping during their G20 meeting in Tokyo, and Trump declared that he had not done so. Yesterday, the Chinese government said that the Canadians were very naive where this dossier is concerned. These are the results of Freeland's strategy, which the prime minister has up to now followed to the letter. After more than seven months of crisis, it's clear that we are no further ahead, on this July 4, 2019.

From my end, I have always claimed that this is not a legal problem, but rather a political problem. First of all, John Bolton, national security adviser for the United States, advised the prime minister of his government's intention to give ten days' notice before demanding the extradition of Ms. Meng, probably to allow the Canadian government to analyze the situation. This was not a legal exchange, but purely political. Later, President Trump himself declared that the Huawei executive was a pawn in the free-trade negotiations with the Chinese government, and that if there was an agreement with President Xi, he was going to withdraw his demand for extradition. You cannot be more political than that.

When Ms. Freeland says that the government has no choice but to follow the rule of law, I would like to reply that she has certainly not read the legislation on extradition, which clearly stipulates that the justice minister can at any time interrupt the procedures before the courts. As well, when there is an extradition judgment against an individual, the authorities cannot proceed without the explicit authorization of the justice minister. So when the foreign affairs minister affirms that the government can do nothing, this is clearly false. And when she declares that the two prisoners in China are not spies, but rather hostages, the Chinese authorities reply that it will be up to the Chinese courts to decide whether Michael Kovrig and Michael Spavor are spies. I presume that if the Chinese government's prosecutors decide they are spies, they will easily find witnesses to back them up. When Canada tells the Chinese that we have no confidence in their system of justice, they will retort that a country that admits to having committed genocide vis-à-vis the Indigenous peoples over the last sixty years cannot seriously claim to give lessons to anyone at all, etc.

When the government consulted me over the last few months, here are the positions I took: I concluded very early on that there was no solution to this problem so long as Meng Wanzhou was detained in Vancouver, and it is, in my opinion, an illusion to believe that the two Canadians will be freed and the economic sanctions removed without this condition being met.

A first solution, implicating the government less, in my opinion, would be to allow Ms. Meng, already free on bail, to return home to China, and to come back to Canada for the start of her trial. On the principle of reciprocity, the Chinese could offer the same thing to the two Canadian prisoners, that is to release them on bail and let them return to Canada, pending their trials in China. Of course, it's not certain that the three people would, in fact, present themselves for the trials, but the problem would at least be solved in the short term.

A second solution would be to proceed to an exchange of "spies," as is done from time to time in the United States. It's not an ideal plan, but it acknowledges the political nature of the problem, without any other likely outcome than a ruling that is also of a political nature.

Finally, a third solution would be to tell President Trump that if he does not withdraw his demand for Ms. Meng's extradition, Canada will have no other choice than to free her, because her prolonged detention is severely affecting the economic and political interests of our country. The justice minister would then be forced to use the powers conferred by law to put an end to a situation that has already cost farmers all across the country hundreds of millions of dollars. In addition, the Canadian business community is losing colossal sums each day thanks to the freeze in relations and the degraded commercial climate between the two countries.

In any case, the Americans ought to know that the legal procedures before the Court of First Instance, the Appeal Court, and the Supreme Court, can take years. That means that even if the justice system were to finally decide to extradite Ms. Meng to the United States, it couldn't be done before 2022, 2023, or 2024. Thus, the road chosen by the United States was not the best, and for that reason the economy of their northern neighbour and most important commercial partner has been hemorrhaging ever since December 2018.

13

THE LAUNCH OF
MY STORIES, MY TIMES

I t's Tuesday, October 23, 2018. In two days, I will launch my book *My Stories, My Times* at the Château Laurier, and I am in Montreal, where I will have by the end of the day given nine interviews on radio and television. What fascinates me is the importance in life of the passing of time. It allows you to put events into perspective and to view them from another angle and different points of view. When I emerged from the 1995 referendum, twenty-three years ago, the atmosphere was very difficult for me in Quebec. And so I am astonished to see how kind people are, and sometimes even grateful, to the old warrior I have become at the age of eighty-four. What a change!

My appearance on the television program *Tout le monde en parle* seems to have been a great success. Who would have thought that one day Denise Bombardier would publicly offer me what I took as a compliment in affirming that without my contribution as spokesperson for Pierre Elliott Trudeau's Liberals, René Lévesque would have won the referendum in 1980? That I saved the day during the last week of the second referendum in 1995? That I always won, and that I was the best political animal she'd ever known? Not bad, coming from Denise Bombardier!

Obviously, the conversation became a bit heated when I affirmed that if we spoke French, it was probably because we had refused to join the American Revolution. The American melting pot, "one flag and one language," would likely have had the same effect on us as on Louisiana, where the French language has virtually disappeared. When I spoke about francophones outside Quebec, she claimed that they were in the process of disappearing. As *Tout le monde en parle* has about 1.5 million viewers, probably more than 200,000 of them francophones in the other provinces, Madame Bombardier's words sparked quite an outcry.

Indeed, for more than a million francophones outside Quebec, being told that you're in the process of disappearing is rather shocking. Especially if you know that when the mother country, France, ceded New France to the English with the Treaty of Paris in 1763, all of New France, from Quebec to Louisiana, counted only ninety thousand inhabitants. In Quebec, there were just forty-five thousand francophones, twenty-two times less than those who are fighting for the French language in the nine other provinces and the three northern territories in Canada today. And in Manitoba, to which Madame Bombardier referred, there are more Franco-Manitobans today than there were franco-phones in Quebec in 1763.

The most surprising comment came from the humorist Jean-René Dufort: he told me that during the second referendum, I had been the Sidney Crosby of the occasion, putting the puck in the net at the last minute, just like the famous hockey player from Nova Scotia during Canada's great victory in carrying off the gold medal at the Winter Olympics. To my great surprise, he added that my secret weapon in victory was love. I asked him what he meant by that, to which he replied that the arrival in Montreal of over 100,000 Canadians from the other provinces during the last week of the campaign had persuaded him that the message to Quebecers asking them to remain in the Canadian family was an authentic gesture of love. At the time, many observers said that it was a strategic error on my part. So I was happy to hear that we were mainly in the right to enthusiastically accept Brian Tobin's idea. This was at a time when he was one of my ministers, before becoming premier of Newfoundland and Labrador.

During the nine interviews I granted to the big names of television and radio in Quebec, they were all very civil, even if several among them had in the past been my very severe critics. This is evidence that democracy is thriving in our society, which warms my heart, especially as American "Trump-ery" continues to plague our daily lives.

After the Quebec promotional tour for my book, Random House, the publisher of the English translation, organized, along with interviews with TV and radio journalists, appearances before large book clubs, mostly in Ottawa, Toronto, and Kingston. At each of these public events, there were more than four hundred guests, and every time, I responded to questions from a host and from the audience for more than an hour. On Saturday evening, October 27, due to a terrible storm of snow and freezing rain, the four hundred people who had displaced themselves despite everything, cooled their heels as the host, Jim Munson, senator and former journalist, deftly filled in the time during a long delay.

In the course of one of the Q&As, an audience member's interrogation led me to talk about Quebec and Ontario. As I was in the heart of Loyalist country, in Kingston, its capital, I told them that if the Loyalists were able to seek refuge in Ontario, it was because the Quebecers had refused to join the American Revolution. In fact, when the Americans rose up against English domination, they sent Benjamin Franklin to try to convince the Lower Canada colony to join their revolution, as Louisiana, another French colony, had done. Franklin spent a year in Montreal, striving to persuade those who are today's Quebecers to support the American Revolution. He was even one of the founders of the newspaper the *Gazette*. The Catholic Church was a determining factor in our remaining a member of the British Commonwealth. If not for that, the Canada of those days and a large part of its territory would probably not have been preserved, and Loyalists who wished to maintain their allegiance to the British Crown, instead of seeking refuge in Ontario, eastern Quebec, New Brunswick, and Nova Scotia, would likely have been forced to cross the Atlantic to return to their mother country.

Let us say that it gave me great pleasure to tell the descendants of those Loyalists that they owed a great deal to Quebec's francophones! Thanks to them, and to the Loyalists who did not want to join the American Revolution, today's Canada was, to all intents and purposes, born in that moment.

14

MITCHELL SHARP

On Tuesday, March 19, 2019, the morning papers reported that the polls placed Justin Trudeau's Liberals three points behind Andrew Scheer's Conservatives. When I was asked what would happen in the October election, and I replied that I could not make a prediction, because very often the winner emerges during the election campaign. That is exactly what had happened during the campaign in 2015, when Justin Trudeau started off in third place, but finished the race at the head of a majority government.

How is it that this rising star, not just in Canada but also internationally, had only 32.5 per cent of voter intentions six months from the election? How is it that Andrew Scheer, a leader who is rather mediocre and without charisma, is in a better position than the star of selfies, who struck a chord with young people in places as far off as the Philippines and Thailand? I myself had felt a shiver of pride when a young lawyer in Helsinki, Finland, had said, in the presence of

Bruce Hartley, who works with me, that he was part of Justin's fan club in this Nordic capital city.

My first observation is that Justin Trudeau and his team aspire to be reformists on a grand scale, but their lack of experience for succeeding in that goal is more and more apparent. They say to whoever wants to hear that one of their great successes is in having sidelined the old guard. Now, a political party that has existed for 152 years without ever changing its name has in its baggage a culture that has enabled it to dominate the national political scene since the beginning of Confederation. When I became prime minister in 1993, I had been elected as an MP nine times, sat seventeen years in the cabinet, and been Opposition leader for three additional years, in addition to serving as parliamentary secretary for the prime minister and the minister of finance. Despite all this accumulated experience, I thought it best to surround myself at the centre of things with veterans, inviting my former mentor Mitchell Sharp to become part of my team despite his eighty years, for a compensation of one dollar per year. I assigned him to an office neighbouring mine, and I consulted him on a regular basis. He, who had been deputy minister under the all-powerful C. D. Howe during the administration of Louis St. Laurent, had left his post as deputy minister of trade and commerce under John Diefenbaker on a question of principle, a rare phenomenon in the public service. After a successful stint in the private sector, Mitchell became successively minister of trade and commerce and minister of finance under the administration of

Prime Minister Lester B. Pearson, and then foreign minister in Pierre Elliott Trudeau's cabinet. He was indubitably of the old guard, as they say, but what a guard! Everyone went to consult Mitchell. My principal collaborators saw him regularly, the ministers and members came to seek his advice on all sorts of subjects. Often, highly placed civil servants came to seek his opinion or advice, and sometimes even journalists did.

When I presented a problem to Mitchell, he came back to see me in my office a few hours or a few days later. He always had a smile on his lips, and gave me his opinion while noting that he had consulted some old comrades in arms. For example, he would explain to me that St. Laurent, Mackenzie King, Pearson, or Pierre Trudeau had faced similar problems, and that in my place this is what he would do. He felt he was being useful at his age, and he was perfectly right. As for me, in my moments of reflection before making a difficult decision, I found it extremely beneficial to have the advice of this great man who had served his country with such competence, devotion, and sincerity for decades.

Mitchell ended his career on Parliament Hill at the same time as me, on December 12, 2003, when I presented my resignation to the Governor General. A few months later, on March 19, 2004, he died at the age of ninety-two. His wife told me that his return to Parliament as a special adviser had extended his life by several years. I was happy to have helped him end his days in a way that was not only agreeable, but also very useful.

When I went to the funeral home the day before the service, his son, Noel, informed me that I had paid him five dollars for his first five years of service, but that I'd forgotten to pay him the second five dollars for the following five years. That was the case, because I'd framed the five-dollar bill in 1999 but had not been able to do it each year thereafter, because the paper one-dollar bill no longer existed. And so I took out my chequebook and wrote a cheque for five dollars payable to Mitchell Sharp, with the inscription, "Last Payment." I then made my way to his casket and placed the cheque in the handkerchief pocket of his suit jacket, saying aloud, "Mitchell, here is your last payment for a job well done." Noel asked my permission to keep the cheque as a souvenir. From high in heaven, Mitchell, who loved to laugh, must have appreciated the scene.

Writing these words, I remember that when Mitchell retired as a minister, Prime Minister Pierre Trudeau, who wanted to name a governor general from the Canadian West, offered the post to his most experienced former minister. Sharp bluntly refused the proposal, to the surprise of all those who were in the know. Everyone wondered how it was possible for a Scottish immigrant, Protestant, English speaking, from Winnipeg to refuse to be the representative of the Queen in Canada. And here is the very lucid explanation he gives in his memoirs, titled *Which Reminds Me . . .*, published in 1994:

EXTERNAL AFFAIRS AND THE MONARCHY

I am not an anti-monarchist. If I were a British subject living in the British Isles I would be a staunch defender of the monarchy. I admire Queen Elizabeth, with whom I had the privilege of spending many enjoyable hours in the course of my ministerial activities. I also believe that we should continue to model our system of government on that of Britain. Nor, to make it quite clear where I stand, do I favour the election of a head of state, as the president is elected in the United States. It would be sufficient that the Canadian head of state be selected by the government of the day for a fixed term, with the appointment confirmed by Parliament; in other words, a governor general by another name who would be the head of state not vice-head of state.

I have held these views for some time and was confirmed in them by my ministerial experience, particularly as secretary of state for external affairs.

An official visit was arranged for Governor General and Mrs Michener to the Benelux countries in April 1971. Prime Minister Trudeau asked me, as foreign secretary, to accompany them. We were received most hospitably, and Their Excellencies conducted themselves with grace and dignity. The presence of a governor general of Canada did, however, pose a special problem for our hosts. How was he to be treated—as vice-royalty or as full head of state? Queen Juliana and the government of the Netherlands decided to accord full head-of-state honours, and the Belgians and Luxemburgers followed suit.

These were generous gestures on the part of our hosts, but they illustrate the ambiguity of our institutions from an outsider's point of view. To the people of the Netherlands and Belgium, governors general are colonial officials, such as were appointed in the Netherlands East Indies and in the Congo. Many Dutch and Belgian people probably believed, when they saw our governor general in their midst, that Canada had not yet achieved full independence from Britain. In a private conversation at an official affair in Amsterdam, my dinner partner, a devoted admirer of Canada, didn't think that a visit by the governor general was worthy of us. I agreed.

A similar perplexity occurred during the ministerial visit to Latin America in 1968. Our purpose was to promote the sale of Canadian goods and make political contacts with the governments of those countries. We learned, after the trip was arranged, that Her Majesty would also be visiting some countries of Latin America at the same time. Her visit was intended, among other things, to promote British interests, including the sale of British goods. We couldn't ask Her Majesty to perform the function for Canada that she was performing for Britain on that Latin American trip because the Queen is never recognized as Queen of Canada, except when she is in Canada. When in the United States, for example, she is the Queen of Great Britain and promotes good relations between Britain and the United States.

The resulting confusion became very clear one day during the 1976 Montreal Olympics when Her Majesty visited the games after having spent a few days in the United States. An American reporter who had been with her on the American leg of her trip and who was ignorant of the subtleties of our Constitution, said on Canadian television that the Queen of England was in the stands.

Gradually, step-by-step, the governor general has taken over functions that were previously exercised by the monarch, so that within Canada the governor general is virtually head of state. Nevertheless, constitutionally the governor general is only the representative of the monarch.

Hence my strongly held view that Canada should have its own head of state who is not shared by others. The Queen and her successors could then have a special place as head of the Commonwealth as well as queen or king of Great Britain. In that capacity, the monarch would be received with enthusiasm and acclaim by Canadians in all parts of the country, including places Queen Elizabeth is now reluctant to visit.

My views on the monarchy were well known to my colleagues in both the Pearson and Trudeau cabinets. They were also known to some others. So far, however, I have obviously failed to rally a significant following.

One would think that my views would have appealed to a French Canadian like Trudeau. Perhaps they did. But, he did not act on them. He was prime minister when the monarchy was confirmed in our patriated Constitution.

A few years after I had left the ministry, I was asked by Prime Minister Trudeau to accept appointment as governor general. One of the reasons I declined the honour was my well-known attitude towards the institution.

What a man!

15

G7

It is August 2019. A few days ago, French President Emmanuel Macron received the G7 members in Biarritz, which leads me to share with you some experiences I've had at the annual meetings the Canadian prime minister must attend, whether it be the G7, the G20, UN meetings, NATO, APEC, the Summit of the Americas, the Commonwealth, the Francophonie, and others. They require such preparation and travelling that the time has perhaps come to re-evaluate their frequency and the number of participating countries, which must spend billions of dollars to have "the honour of receiving" not only the political leaders, but a large number of bureaucrats, journalists, and other observers. I could tell you many stories and enumerate the great variety of subjects dealt with over dozens of summits, but I'm going to restrict myself to a few incidents that were not reported in the media.

My first summit was at the initial APEC meeting, which took place just a few days after my election as prime minister, on October 25, 1993. The president of the United States, Bill Clinton, had taken the initiative of summoning the chiefs of state and government leaders of the most important fifteen countries with access to the Pacific Ocean. As soon as I arrived at Blake Island, in the city of Seattle, I met Clinton for the first time. He had been president of the United States for only eight months. To everyone's surprise, at the start of our bilateral conversation, I told him that even if the United States was our closest friend, I did not believe, personally, that I should come across as too loyal an ally. "If I'm not too close to you, Mr. President, I will not be seen as the fifty-first American state, and in certain instances, I could do more for you than the CIA itself."

Everyone present seemed taken aback by this declaration, but I had observed that during the Vietnam War, Prime Minister Pearson had kept his distance from President Lyndon B. Johnson. Prime Minister Pierre Elliott Trudeau had done the same with President Ronald Reagan. I had also seen that my predecessor, Brian Mulroney, who was very close to Reagan and George Bush Sr., made Canadians uneasy, as they viewed and considered themselves independent of our southern neighbours. Even if I became Bill Clinton's good friend, he understood well this desire for independence during the seven years we collaborated, and it was the same thing with George W. Bush, who grasped perfectly my position when Canada refused to participate in the Iraq war. It was the first time that Canadians did not join in a war in which the United States and Great Britain were actively involved.

In July 1994, I participated in my first G7 summit in Naples, in the south of Italy, where we were sumptuously received by the ineffable Prime Minister Silvio Berlusconi. In discussion for three days with the august political leaders of the United States, France, Great Britain, Germany, Japan, and Italy, I felt very distant from the village of Baie-de-Shawinigan, which had seen me born sixty years earlier. When you are only six or eight around the table, no one is going to read a text prepared by bureaucrats; the discussion is, for the most part, informal, direct, lively, and inevitably more productive. At the time, the G7 was a summit designed to discuss economic matters, and was not the political management board it is today, where you talk about everything with twenty other leaders, who are invited as observers with or without a formal status as participant.

For the first evening of the Naples summit, Prime Minister Berlusconi had invited his guests to a lavish dinner. President Clinton was late as usual for the reception, which also delayed the arrival of French President François Mitterrand due to the order of precedence. The rest of us had to wait more than an hour for Clinton's arrival, followed less than two minutes later by that of Mitterrand. Because the G7 presidents, according to protocol, are given preferential treatment, Clinton and Mitterrand had priority over the prime ministers. And since Mitterrand had priority over Clinton, having been a member of the G7 for thirteen years, he wanted to appear last at the dinner. Bill's tardiness forced Mitterrand to meander for an hour through the neighbouring streets before arriving last, because for him, precedence was a sacred principle.

Germany was represented by a very impressive personage, Chancellor Helmut Kohl, who was the architect of German unification and the prime mover behind the single currency, the euro. During a break, we talked about the departure of Mitterrand, and we had both been very impressed by the performance of Jacques Delors, who represented the European Union. We knew that his name figured among the candidates to replace Mitterrand as the socialist leader leading up to the next French presidential election. Helmut invited me to help exert pressure on Jacques Delors, telling him that he would make a superb French president. So here is the picture: we have the leader of the German right and the Canadian Liberal leader urging Jacques Delors to agree to be the leader of the left in France—surprising but true.

As this was Mitterrand's fourteenth and last summit, the final lunch was devoted to thanking the French president for his great contribution to the advancement of the Western world. Since it was a meeting with no other purpose, as is often the case in such circumstances, history became the subject of conversation, and at a certain point I said that if French Lower Canada had joined with the seven American states during the War of Independence against England, the French tongue would probably have become the official language of the United States.

Following its independence, the American Congress had voted to retain the English language, but as Louisiana and

Quebec would have represented a quarter of the American states, French would probably have won out, since Thomas Jefferson and John Adams had both been ambassadors to Paris and had cultivated French support on their way to breaking free from Great Britain. The Frenchman La Fayette's role during that period is well known. I could imagine Mitterrand contemplating this possibility. It was then that Bill Clinton remarked, with humour, that if history had followed that path, he would be there not as president, but as a note taker for me! That was Bill Clinton for you—a great charmer.

The next summit took place in Halifax in 1995, and as host, I was responsible for ensuring that it went well. In addition to the amazing Nova Scotian hospitality we enjoyed, this was the last innocent summit where we, state and government leaders, did not resemble prisoners surrounded by guardians armed to the teeth. At a certain point, Clinton, Chirac, Kohl, Yeltsin, and the other leaders mingled with the enthusiastic crowds on the Halifax streets. Also, this was the first time the G7 became a G8, as Russia, represented by Boris Yeltsin, participated in the three-day meeting.

To honour my guests, we attended a magnificent performance by the Cirque du Soleil. A British member of the Cirque team had asked to see me to inquire as to whether he might be able to meet John Major, because the father of the prime minister of Great Britain had been a friend and workmate of his own father. That was done, and it was very moving to hear this circus worker tell the prime minister of his country that his father had, like himself, laboured in this industry all his life. It was an extraordinary meeting, and interesting to hear the British prime minister talking about his father's career in such a demanding profession.

John told me after the meeting that his father's work was so hard, he had taken steps to emigrate to Canada. One of the two friends' sons had followed in his father's footsteps in the circus industry, while the other became prime minister of a great and important country, and they both met at the G8 summit in Halifax. It was fascinating to realize that most of my G8 colleagues had had modest beginnings. Chirac, like Kohl, was the son of a municipal bureaucrat, Yeltsin was the son of a farmer, and Clinton was not yet born when his father died in a car accident; he had lived in poverty. As for me, I am the son of a machinist.

The G8 summit in Lyon in 1996 took us to one of the regions in France where you eat particularly well and have access to wines that are among the finest in the world. Raymond Barre, former prime minister of France and mayor of the G8's host city, made sure that the meals were extraordinarily good, prepared by the region's greatest chefs, and that the wines were up to the occasion. And so imagine his reaction when he was told that Chirac, Kohl, and Yeltsin, and perhaps Clinton as well, were accompanying these feasts with beer rather than the superb burgundies. Jacques Chirac, president of France, drank only beer and not a drop of wine!

The following year, during the summit in Cologne, under the presidency of Gerhard Schröder, rumour had it that Russian President Boris Yeltsin would not be present, as his health was very fragile. Despite the rumours, he arrived in the meeting room only a few minutes late. As I was sitting to his left, I greeted him by putting my hand on his right shoulder. He grabbed it tightly, and to amuse himself, began dragging me toward him. It all turned into a kind of arm wrestle, because I followed his lead with vigour, impelling Bill Clinton to say, "Look at the two polar bears squabbling at the other end of the table!" The photographers took a number of photos, showing that Boris still had a lot of energy. Enjoying the competition, I gave it my all, and the match ended in a tie. There was no more speculation concerning the health of "Russia's polar bear."

During the Genoa G8, the Italian authorities, fearing the disruption of street demonstrations, had a very original idea. Instead of hosting the delegations in hotels, two high-end cruise ships were rented and anchored in the port, concentrating in one location the delegations' lodgings and offices.

When my turn came to host my second G7 summit in 2002, instead of holding it in a city, I decided to set it in Kananaskis, a resort centre in the Rocky Mountains, west of Calgary. Because the number of hotels is necessarily limited in such a site, it was impossible to accommodate all the delegations. And so we decided to limit each one to forty members. Imagine the outcry from the American authorities! Generally, the American delegation at a G7 meeting is composed of about a thousand people. The Americans told us that it was impossible for them to agree to that site. It should be said that the Japanese also came with a delegation as impressive as that of our neighbours to the south. My sherpa Claude Laverdure told me that we were at an impasse. So I decided to call George W. Bush to ask him why he needed a thousand advisers for a meeting of eight heads of state and government, when I felt that forty were sufficient for each one of us. One of George W. Bush's qualities is that he doesn't, as it were, beat around the bush. He replied that indeed that might be too many for his purposes, but to be present at the G8 was doubtless important for the resumés of hundreds of bureaucrats. Still, at the end of the day, he was in total agreement with me. I don't know how many Americans arrived in Calgary, but they were kept about a hundred kilometres from the meeting of heads of state and government leaders.

That was a very successful summit. My guests were most happy to spend a few days in the renowned Canadian Rockies. The police in Calgary didn't have many problems because our location was very remote. The only sour note I remember was that the police who were protecting us had to shoot a bear that was venturing too close to where we sat. (By the way, the only G7 hosted by Stephen Harper and the Conservatives took place in Muskoka in 2010, and it cost twice as much as the Kananaskis summit.)

While we were in government, Canada was involved in a mushrooming of annual meetings for heads of state and government leaders. In 1993, I was at the first meeting of APEC in Seattle for countries of the Pacific. In 1995, we invited the Russian president to Halifax, altering the G7 to a G8. In 1999, we participated in the Summit of the Americas, in

Miami. The G7 was conceived as an economic forum, but over time the discussions shifted to other topics, such as peace, conflicts, hunger, the environment, and so on. My minister of finance and I always thought that it would be useful to hold a summit of finance ministers to discuss only economic problems. That became the G20 of finance ministers.

Soon after its creation, the G20 of finance ministers became the G20 of heads of state and government leaders. Now, during the G7 meeting, the host invites fifteen other countries to participate, after a fashion, in the G7. The host of the G20 does the same thing, and the G20 has thus become a kind of G40 for heads of state.

As I wrote earlier, when we are seven or eight around a table, no one reads long texts prepared by bureaucrats, and the discussion is direct, interesting, productive. However, the more the number of players increases, the more the attention of those present diminishes, and during long meetings I've often seen participants doing crossword puzzles or playing cards on their tablets.

And so I really ask myself whether government leaders should not reduce the number of these summits. Rather than changing countries every year, they should perhaps hold them always in the same place, at the United Nations headquarters in Geneva, for example, or on a large cruise ship, as the Italians did in Genoa in 2001, in order to better manage security in the event of violent demonstrations. The cost imposed on each host, sometimes reaching a billion dollars, would be greatly reduced and possibly shared. The grumbling, especially of those I call the "professional protesters," would lose its allure, and instead of heading out to stir things up, they would just go off to work.

What is more, I believe that this proliferation of summits does enormous damage to the effectiveness of the United Nations. Twenty years ago, the opening of the UN General Assembly was a major event for the political and journalistic class. Today, it has become a mundane banality, and the moral authority of the United Nations, sadly, continues to decline.

16

HONG KONG AND TIANANMEN SQUARE

It's Sunday, April 17, 2019, and early this morning I received a phone call from Tung Chee-hwa, who became the first administrator of Hong Kong when the British surrendered its colony to China. For several weeks, the demonstrations in the streets of the richest territory in Asia have been riveting and unsettling. I was there at the beginning of July 2018, and even if all was calm during my five-day stay, you could sense the tension. The conference of Chinese and American businesspeople had even been obliged, under the circumstances, to switch hotels. Tung Chee-hwa, a very important businessman in the time of the British, left the direction of his large family business to become the leader of this territory that had once more become Chinese, and all agree that he performed a demanding task very well.

After my conversations with Tung Chee-hwa and his friends, I had a better understanding of the situation. As is often the case, it all began with an incident that would normally have been only a small news item. A Hong Kong resident had gone to Taiwan to marry a woman in that territory. Not very nice, he killed his new wife during their honeymoon. Before the police could arrest him, he hopped on a plane to return to Hong Kong. The Taiwan police wanted to bring him back to put him on trial and asked the Hong Kong government to return the murderer. Given the regime of "one country, two systems" for external affairs, the authority in this matter rested with Beijing. This whole juridical muddle forced the Hong Kong authorities to adopt a law permitting the extradition of their citizens to Greater China, which triggered the protests with which you are familiar.

This Chinese problem made the front pages of Western newspapers, and everyone feared a new Tiananmen Square. I hope that the Chinese will not repeat the tragedy of 1989, but that is yet to be seen.

As for me, when I organized my first Team Canada mission in November 1994, I went to China with the provincial premiers and five hundred businesspeople and scholars. The Canadian delegation was the most impressive in number to have ever visited China.

Along with the premiers, I was received by President Jiang Zemin, and we had as our host Prime Minister Li Peng, of sad renown, as he was held responsible for the Tiananmen massacre. To everyone's surprise, he conducted himself like a perfect gentleman. He participated in several of our meetings and took our visit seriously. His government apparatus could not have been more efficient, businesspeople signed billion-dollar contracts, and China bought from us two CANDU nuclear reactors also worth billions of dollars. Li Peng even sent his son, an electrical engineer, to study the CANDU system in Toronto. All the members of the enormous Canadian delegation were more than happy, and the media concluded that the visit was a great success. During the period when I was prime minister, we organized another Team Canada every year. Everywhere we went, we represented the largest delegation of its kind to visit countries in the four corners of the world.

As was appropriate, I invited China's president and prime minister to visit Canada, and they both in fact came: Prime Minister Li Peng in October 1995, and President Jiang Zemin in November 1997.

In the course of these bilateral meetings with Prime Minister Li Peng, I had the occasion to discuss with him what had happened in Tiananmen Square. He was frustrated to be shouldered with the blame, he told me, because it was President Deng Xiaoping's government that had decided to put an end to what Deng saw as the beginning of a counter-revolution that could grow into a civil war. Li Peng told me that he was not the decision maker and did not deserve the bad publicity he'd received. He also introduced me to members of his family, one of whom is the minister of transport in today's Chinese government. His wife acted as Aline's hostess. She was a kind woman who was so endearing that Aline showed her photos of our grandchildren. When she took hold of the photo of our grandson Maximilien, she seemed dazzled to see this lovely boy with very curly hair, something that's rare in China. She said to Aline, "He should marry my granddaughter."

As Prime Minister Li Peng was a perfect host to me and the provincial premiers, it was natural to invite him to visit Canada. He had accepted with pleasure the invitation of the provincial premiers and myself, but things became more complicated when the time came for his visit. Before arriving in Canada, he'd visited Germany, where given the size of the demonstrations, he'd decided to cut short his stay. The same thing happened when he went to Mexico.

When he came to Canada, everyone anticipated a trip not much different from that to Germany and Mexico. The delegation first made an unofficial stop in Halifax, without any incident. When he arrived in Ottawa, we chose the Lester B. Pearson Building, where the Department of Foreign Affairs was housed, to hold our bilateral talks. There were some fairly small demonstrations on Parliament Hill, without the Chinese being aware of them. For the main reception and the formal dinner, we chose the Sheraton Hotel in Montreal. The Chinese arrived at the hotel toward the end of the afternoon, and everything went well. As we had invited the provincial premiers and a goodly number of businesspeople who had been part of Team Canada, we were all in a large reception hall when the famous Prime Minister Li Peng arrived.

Everything was going swimmingly, when suddenly, just as we were going to sit down to our meal, the Chinese prime minister's private secretary, livid, confronted Jean Pelletier, my right-hand man, to say that there was a large number of protesters in the street, on the hotel's ground floor. While I was in conversation with Prime Minister Li Peng, Pelletier and his counterpart advised us of the situation. I immediately went with my guest into the next room, where we indeed heard noises coming from the street. I approached the window, looked down, and saw placards, but as we were on the fortieth floor, I couldn't see what they said, and the noise was not that loud. I then turned to my guest and joked that as usual, the people in the street were protesting against me. He burst out laughing, returned to the reception room, ate with us, and made his speech to the three hundred guests. All ended well.

After a night's rest, with his visit complete, he left as planned, to the great relief of the Chinese ambassador to Canada and Canada's ambassador to China. When we made our second visit to China with Team Canada, Li Peng was still prime minister of his country, and we all, the provincial premiers and the five hundred other Canadians who accompanied us, were received with the same courtesies.

Li Peng died a few weeks ago. Despite his efforts at rehabilitation, all the Western press spoke of him as the "Butcher of Tiananmen Square," without ever examining his long career. By contrast, his death was an important event in China. They talked of the "adopted son" of Prime Minister Zhou Enlai, of his long career in the Chinese Communist Party, and above all, for them, he had become the hero of Tiananmen Square. He had avoided counter-revolution in a country of 1.3 billion citizens. Two perspectives that are utterly different for two worlds destined to work together for a very long time. Whether we like it or not, for the Western world, he will always be the "Butcher of Tiananmen Square."

17

THE JOURNALISTS

O ften, people ask me if I would survive in politics today with instant modes of communication on multiple platforms replacing the more traditional ones of my forty years of public life, when newspapers, radio, and television doled out their information at predictable intervals every day, rather than in the 24-hour cycle on the internet now favoured by those under thirty years old. I can only answer: maybe yes, maybe no.

When I first started out, in the years 1956 to 1958, as a member of the Liberal Party with its nerve centres for student Liberals, whether in the riding or at university or nationally, the newspapers were dominant, radio was less important, and television was in its infancy. The notion of spontaneous interviews, first at the radio microphones and then on television, represented an unsettling innovation for politicians. Very soon, the House of Commons debates being broadcast live on television utterly changed the feeling of those exchanges. Despite its initial discomfort, the political class adapted. I believe that today's transformations will alter certain attitudes in the political class, but as in the years from 1950 to 1960, in the end, the desire for and the necessity of having a healthy democracy will impose adjustments on all sides.

Often, when I meet with journalists, some confess that they miss the availability, spontaneity, and humour I brought to the table. I reply that the relationship between journalists and politicians has radically changed. To illustrate the point, here are a few stories that come to mind.

First, in the rapport between politicians and journalists, there was once a rule of confidentiality that was adhered to on either side: if we said to a journalist that the conversation was confidential, it really was confidential. "Off the record" was respected as a genuine code of honour. As a result, journalists had a great deal of influence, because ministers and MPs discussed openly the nation's problems with journalists who were serious and experienced. For example, Bruce Hutchison, the head editorialist for the *Vancouver Sun*, came to Ottawa for a week twice a year, and he was received by the prime minister, the ministers, opposition party leaders, MPs, senators—basically, all those he wanted to see, eagerly received him. He shared his opinions freely, and everyone greatly appreciated his company. His views were reflected in legislation and discussions. In fact, he had more influence than the ministers and MPs from the West. His equivalent in French Canada was Claude Ryan, director of *Le Devoir*, who scrupulously obeyed the rule of confidentiality. Everyone held him in high esteem and consulted him. He learned a great deal from his conversations with veteran politicians, and his opinions were routinely discussed around the cabinet table.

There was also Jean-Marc Poliquin, a highly respected Radio-Canada journalist who came from my region and who was a former assistant to Noël Dorion, a minister in John Diefenbaker's cabinet. I had the privilege of benefiting from his vast experience in journalism and politics. In 1968, as a brand-new minister of Indian affairs and northern development, I was in Paris, and on my schedule I read "visit to the France-Canada Chamber of Commerce." I learned in the car that this was not just a simple visit, but that I had to make a speech in front of 150 people. I'm in Paris, a new thirty-four-year-old minister, I've never spoken before "real Frenchmen," and I've just learned what I have to do. There was no getting out of it, and I was, as they say in Mauricie, *paniqué ben raide*, or scared stiff.

On my arrival, I met Jean-Marc, who was then the Radio-Canada correspondent in Paris. I took him aside to share my panic. He said, "Jean, calm down, and when you get up to speak, pretend that you're in front of the La Tuque Chamber of Commerce; talk about the Indians, the Eskimos, the great Canadian North, as simply as possible, and all will be well." That's exactly what I did, and to my great surprise, it was a success. Jean-Marc Poliquin got me out of a bind and gave me some advice that has stood me in good stead for the rest of my life: never panic!

I believe that during my entire career, my relations with the press were quite good. I told myself that like me in the world of politics, they have a job to do, and freedom of the press is the strength of democracy. Without a free press, there's totalitarianism. In my opinion, you shouldn't call journalists too often to complain, unless the information being conveyed is false. When there was a difference of opinion, I told myself that the readers would make their own judgments. That is freedom of the press. Sometimes, frustrated, I would say to a journalist, "If you're so smart, why not run in an election, and then we'll see what the people think of you!" But I didn't do that very often . . .

One day, the *Globe and Mail* published a story on the front page with a big headline that took me to task. In question period, I offered explanations that calmed the storm. The next morning, the *Globe and Mail* published nothing at all about my presentation to the House of Commons. Angry, and counter to my usual practices, I phoned the publisher of the *Globe and Mail* to ask for an explanation. He told me that his paper had not printed my clarification because there was no one around at that time to translate my words from French into English. I said to him, "If I'd confessed to making a big mistake, I'm sure you would have found someone to translate what I said in the House of Commons, and once again put the story on the front page. I should be taking you to court!" To which he replied, "Is that a threat?" Trapped, I answered, "It's not a threat; it's a promise!"

The next day, I asked my friend Pierre Genest, a prominent francophone lawyer in Toronto, twice elected president of the Ontario Bar Association, to launch legal proceedings against the *Globe and Mail*. Two years later, the paper decided to settle out of court, and since I'd had a cabinet promotion, I was awarded punitive damages of only five thousand dollars, because, in fact, no damage had been done to me. Pierre sent the cheque in Aline's name, telling her to do what she wanted with the money, because Jean didn't deserve a thing. With the money, Aline bought herself a piano, and when we received visitors, I introduced them to my children and the *Globe and Mail* piano. It's a story that still amuses our guests.

During the 1993 election, which resulted in my being named prime minister, my friend Guy Suzor, one of my key collaborators going far back in time in my riding, informed me three months before the vote that he'd learned that a very unfavourable poll in Saint-Maurice would be published a few days prior to the election. Indeed, five days before the vote, headlines in Montreal's *La Presse* and Trois-Rivières' *Le Nouvelliste* referred to a poll indicating that I would be beaten in my own riding. Since I easily won the riding in the end, and also the entire country, on the day after the election on October 26, 1993, I appeared before the Ottawa journalists at my first press conference, brandishing the two newspapers with big headlines forecasting my defeat. It was a little like what President Harry Truman did when he appeared before the American press, which had proclaimed on the front page, the day after his victory, the election of his Republican opponent, Governor Thomas Dewey.

I then had this photo framed, showing me as the new prime minister holding up the headlines of *La Presse* and *Le Nouvelliste* predicting my defeat in my riding. I showed it to André Desmarais, the husband of my daughter, France, president of *La Presse* and responsible for *Le Nouvelliste*, and I said, "André, here is how much influence you have over your papers; here is what they did to your father-in-law!" Clearly, Power Corporation respected their journalists' freedom. Some would say a bit too much, but not me!

These days, journalists like to say that President Trump never says sorry, and that Prime Minister Trudeau apologizes too often. But how is it for the journalists? Many of them are reluctant to retract anything, even when they get things wrong, and here are two examples concerning the well-respected *Le Devoir*.

When I won my case against Justice John Gomery and the federal court obliged him to remove references to me from his report, a *Le Devoir* journalist wrote that this was just what he expected, because Justice Max Teitelbaum had been named to the federal court by my government. One of my acquaintances contacted the paper to point out that in fact Teitelbaum was named by Brian Mulroney's Conservative government, and that in that light the insinuation of a bias in my favour did not hold water. Neither the open letter correcting the facts nor any form of rectification was ever published. As well, the federal government appealed the decision of the judge of first instance, and three judges of the Court of Appeal unanimously confirmed the earlier decision. The three judges who heard the appeal had also been named to the federal Court of Appeal by Brian Mulroney's government. But none of that was considered worthy of a correction. What, then, would it have taken?

Obviously, I could talk about dozens of other cases, but here is one that didn't involve me but is very interesting. Jean Charest's government, facing difficulties with Quebec's justice system, asked former Supreme Court justice Michel Bastarache to preside over a commission of inquiry. Justice Bastarache, a former judge of the New Brunswick Court of Appeal and the first Acadian to be named to the Supreme Court of Canada, had just retired, but he accepted the mandate. One day, *Le Devoir* published an article claiming that the government had bought Justice Bastarache a Mercedes, and that he was a Liberal and a friend of Jean Charest. Understandably offended, the judge informed the paper that he'd owned the Mercedes for years, that he had never been a member of the Liberal Party, and that he'd never met Jean Charest. Once again, the paper neither offered a retraction nor published any correction. Distressing.

All professions produce good and bad practitioners. The press and journalism are no exceptions. In the course of the four decades of my public life, I've always said that freedom of the press is essential to democracy, and I have good memories of my relations with journalists. It always gives me pleasure to talk about some of them that life's hazards have set in my path. In this respect, we are luckier in Canada than in the United States. Imagine the predicament of American journalists who must deal with a president who, according to the *Washington Post*, lied more than ten thousand times in less than three years!

During my entire career, I met a large number of journalists who genuinely sought to write the truth, inspired by the model of integrity and professionalism represented by the great Walter Cronkite. It was he who wrote that at the start of his career as a young journalist in Kansas City, there were two papers so concerned about their reputations that if one of them wrote that Mr. White had done something, when his name was actually spelled *Whyte*, the competitor highlighted the error, however small, with pleasure in its next day's paper. It's clear that Donald Trump was not trained at Walter Cronkite's school.

Shortly after I set down the words above regarding my relations with journalists being in general cordial, respectful, and sometimes even friendly, I received a touching message from a press gallery veteran, Anthony Wilson-Smith:

Sir: I ran into Peter Donolo recently—which reminded me that I have been meaning to write this note to you for some time.

In going through my old Ottawa-related files, I recently came across several articles I wrote in my *Maclean's* days that now, to be frank, cause me some embarrassment. In the first case, I criticized you at the time of the U.S. invasion of Iraq for your apparent "waffling" on whether Canada should join in the conflict. It is now clear, of course, that the invasion of Iraq came under false pretenses and was a bad idea in any circumstances; through your excellent political instincts, you saved countless Canadian lives by ensuring we did not take place in a pointless conflict that continues to cause problems to this day. In the second instance, I was one of those who suggested it was time for you to step down some months before you announced that decision yourself. Again, I was wrong in doing so: history already shows you to be one of our most successful prime ministers. We were privileged to have you in office for as long as possible.

Fortunately, you have never been guided by the views of journalists like myself. But you have always been gracious and thoughtful in our exchanges over the years, and I have tremendous respect for you as well as personal affection. Canada is a much better country for your wisdom and years of service—and I want to be on record along with many, many other Canadians in acknowledging that.

I wish you continuing health and good fortune over Christmas and far beyond—and thank you again on a personal note for the courtesy you have always shown me.

Best wishes
Tony Wilson-Smith
Anthony Wilson-Smith, President and CEO,
Historica Canada

Helmut Schmidt, former chancellor of Germany and founder of the InterAction Council, an organization that brings together former chiefs of state and government leaders, which I had the honour of presiding over.

"Two polar bears," joked Bill Clinton, seeing me with Boris Yeltsin, president of Russia.

A visit to Baffin Island with Jacques Chirac, president of France, and his wife, Bernadette.

Max Gros-Louis, grand chief of the Huron-Wendat Nation in Wendake, at the unveiling of my official portrait.

The actor Leslie Nielsen, and his wife, Barbaree. His brother Erik Nielsen was a Yukon MP.

Nelson Mandela, whom I made an honorary Canadian citizen in 2001.

Chancellor Helmut Kohl, the man who reunified Germany.

In a serious conversation with George H. W. Bush.

Kofi Annan, secretary general of the United Nations.

A rare privilege: a private audience with Pope John Paul II.

Mitchell Sharp, to whom I owe an enormous debt.

Tony Blair, prime minister of the United Kingdom, standing before a famous photograph of Winston Churchill by the great Yousuf Karsh.

Yitzhak Rabin, prime minister of Israel. The same day in November 1995 that he was assassinated, an intruder tried to assassinate me, as well, in my home. That day, my wife, Aline, saved my life.

Her Majesty, Queen Elizabeth II, during a state dinner.

18

MINORITY GOVERNMENTS

It's Saturday afternoon, October 19, 2019, and I've returned from a political meeting in the riding of the excellent environment minister Catherine McKenna. This is the last speech I will give during this election campaign. I'll have visited five provinces and twelve different ridings. A few months ago, I wrote that this election would produce a Liberal minority government. Today, only two days before the election, and after this tour of the West Coast and Nova Scotia, I have not changed my mind: it really will be a Liberal minority government. Of course, I could always be wrong.

For some days, citizens and journalists have been asking me how the next government will work. I reply that Canada has been led by minority governments nine times since the election of John Diefenbaker's Conservatives in 1957, re-elected with another minority in 1962. Lester B. Pearson and the Liberals formed very productive governments in 1963 and 1965 even if they were minorities. I participated in a very interesting minority government with Pierre Elliott Trudeau between 1972 and 1974, when the New Democrat David Lewis held the balance of power. Then Joe Clark and his Progressive Conservatives formed a minority government that lasted nine months in 1979 to 1980. When Paul Martin became leader of the Liberal Party in 2003, he formed a minority government in 2004 after his first election, and Stephen Harper was later prime minister of two consecutive minority governments. In the course of the last twenty elections in which I participated, nine produced minority governments, and I was in the government during three of them, two with Pearson and one with Trudeau as prime minister. I also served in the Opposition when Joe Clark became prime minister.

It is remarkable that with these nine minority governments, we've never had a coalition. To survive each confidence vote, the government had to find a formula to rally enough votes from the two or three opposition parties in order to gain a majority. During Lester B. Pearson's first minority government, I was his parliamentary secretary, and I was seriously involved in the strategy being developed to obtain the support of the Créditistes, who were largely from Quebec. Their de facto leader was Réal Caouette, the member from Rouyn-Noranda, but who was born in my electoral riding. With each throne speech and each budget, we had to agree to some of Réal's propositions, as we called them, so he could claim some kind of victory. Sometimes, when no adequate accommodation emerged, it turned out that "by chance" a certain number of MPs from the three parties forming the opposition found themselves outside of the nation's capital, either in their ridings or on a parliamentary mission abroad, or simply sick for a period of time.

In the 1960s, it was not only the speech from the throne and the budgets that required the House's confidence, but all the government's projects, which kept it constantly on its guard. For the first time in our parliamentary history, it was Réal Caouette who established that to lose the vote on a government bill did not necessarily imply a loss of confidence in the House of Commons. We were studying the third reading of a government bill to put into effect the 1968 budget presented by Mitchell Sharp, then finance minister. At that time, Parliament was in session every Monday, Tuesday, and Thursday evenings, until ten o'clock. As I was minister of national revenue, I was helping the finance minister with the bill. It had been agreed by the House leaders of each party that the vote on third reading would take place that night. The whips of each party had calculated the members who would be present for the vote.

At about nine o'clock, as planned, the bell sounded to call the members to their seats in order to record their votes. In a minority situation, we, the Liberals, had the responsibility of winning the vote. Sharp was informed by the whip that everything was under control and that he did not have to be concerned about the situation. But by chance, or perhaps not, three Conservative members who were supposed to be absent turned up, and we lost the vote on third reading by one vote.

As soon as the House speaker announced the result, the Conservatives celebrated the government's defeat, tossing sheets of paper in the air, proclaiming victory, and defying us to go before the electorate.

On the cabinet bench, we were in a state of shock, stunned, disoriented. Faced with this terrible commotion, the great parliamentarian Allan MacEachen saved the day. Despite the deafening noise, he was able to attract the attention of the speaker and propose an adjournment of the House, which Leader of the Opposition Robert Stanfield accepted, to the great chagrin of John Diefenbaker, who insisted that this was a vote of confidence, that there was no more government, and that Prime Minister Pearson had to ask the Governor General to call an election. It was then that Réal Caouette, leader of the Créditistes, asserted that the bill had been defeated, but not the government, something that was utterly new and without precedent in British-inspired parliaments.

The next day, MacEachen presented a motion of confidence, which was approved with the support of Réal Caouette's Créditistes. Mitchell Sharp proposed changes in his bill that were approved by the House. And so the deputy from Rouyn-Noranda saved Lester B. Pearson's Liberal government's skin, and changed the tradition according to which the loss of a vote on legislation presented by the government signalled its defeat and led automatically to the dissolution of Parliament and the calling of general elections. Since Caouette's intervention, all the minority governments of Joe Clark, Pierre Elliott Trudeau, Paul Martin, as well as the two of Stephen Harper have respected the precedent established in 1968 by Réal Caouette, born in Saint-Théophile, near Lac-à-la-Tortue, on the outskirts of Shawinigan.

Parliamentary rules continue to evolve, as much in Canada as in Australia and Great Britain. It's possible that the recent change introduced during the alliance of the Liberal Democrats in the U.K. Parliament with David Cameron's Conservatives fundamentally changed the meaning of a responsible government in a British-inspired parliament. To protect themselves from a hasty election that Cameron might call, the Liberal Democrats demanded a law declaring that a prime minister could not call an election without the approval of two-thirds of the members. This legislation utterly altered the tradition, and now a prime minister's loss of confidence is not enough to trigger a general election. We've been able to observe the new system in operation among our English cousins since the debate on Brexit. We saw former prime minister Theresa May lose vote after vote for a year and yet remain in power.

It's even worse under the new British prime minister. Boris Johnson has not won a single vote in the U.K. Parliament. It is ten days from the October 31 deadline, and Parliament does not want to support a single law on the subject. It's unprecedented: the British government has not had the confidence of Parliament for a year, and it does not resign or call an election. I'm very curious to know how all that will end.

As for me, I like to make people smile when they talk to me about minority government, telling them that what has lacked in my political career is the challenge of having to lead that form of government. It is at once the worst and the best to be faced in our parliamentary system. In any case, it will not be me shouldering the task as of next Tuesday, October 22, 2019.

19

ALBERTA, ITS OIL, AND CANADA

On August 5, 2019, I read an interesting article by Joël-Denis Bellavance in *La Presse+* describing the state of mind of Albertans, who seem to accept the proposition of their new premier, Jason Kenney, that if Justin Trudeau is elected in October, Alberta should separate from the rest of Canada. The subject, of course, caught my interest, because I've lived through two referendums, in 1980 and 1995, on the separation of Quebec, presented with two questions whose clarity was certainly not their primary characteristic. During the first referendum, Prime Minister Pierre Trudeau gave me the responsibility of leading the federal troops, and during the second, I was prime minister of Canada. These consultations deeply marked the history of our country, and I would like to share with you some reflections on that subject, because in fact, since the end of the colonial regimes in Africa and the dismantlement of the Soviet Union, there have not been many new countries on the roster of the United Nations.

First of all, separate or not, Alberta will always be a land-locked territory, whose principal problem is its incapacity to construct new pipelines to transport its oil to markets. During the nine years of Albertan Stephen Harper's mandate as prime minister, not an inch of new pipeline saw the light, not leading to the Pacific, nor the Atlantic, nor the United States. Justin Trudeau did allow the construction of the Keystone XL pipeline to take Albertan oil toward Texas, even if it was blocked by environmentalists and the Indigenous population in the Midwestern states. In addition, the Texas refineries are much less interested in buying Canadian oil, because our neighbours to the south now have a surplus of oil, making them exporters. And so even if Trudeau gave them permission to come and get our oil, they're not really interested, and that's not the Liberals' fault. But Trudeau did authorize the construction of the pipeline going south, something the Harper government avoided doing during its three mandates in power.

As for carrying oil toward the Pacific, since the beginning of his mandate Trudeau has asserted that he had to diversify markets and increase the transport capacity toward the West Coast. He was met with systematic resistance from British Columbia, mostly from the New Democratic government in a coalition with the Green Party. In addition, there were loud protests from ecologists and hundreds of Indigenous groups. And British Columbia's government took court action against the federal government. The nasty feds won in court but now had to take billions of dollars out of the pockets of all Canadian taxpayers to buy the existing pipeline, because the American owners did not want to double the capacity of the oil route leading to the Pacific Ocean. Instead of thanking Trudeau for buying the pipeline to the Pacific and investing billions of Canadian taxpayers' dollars, Alberta's Conservative government and the federal Conservatives blamed Trudeau's government for having voted in a law that would protect the magnificent Pacific coastline from the catastrophes that might arise as a result of the increase in traffic of oil tankers coming to collect Alberta's oil, aggravating the risk of polluting the British Columbia seashores. If oil is essential to Alberta, the spectacular beauty of those shores belonging to our province that gives onto the Pacific Ocean is also of prime importance to the citizens of British Columbia and the rest of Canada.

As for the proposed pipeline that would transport oil from Alberta toward the country's East Coast, it's true that many people in Quebec oppose it, but the federal government has not had to make a decision as they did in British Columbia, because the group that initiated the project withdrew it themselves for economic reasons linked to the low price of oil on the international market. However, Alberta Premier Jason Kenney came to protest in Montreal and proposed a referendum back home to eliminate transfer payments, which cannot be done without a process as complicated as a constitutional amendment.

And so, rather than inveighing against Quebec, Mr. Kenney should perhaps recognize that Quebecers are now buying about 60 per cent of their oil from Alberta, whereas in the past it was only 20; that Ontarians are forced to buy their oil from Alberta because of the Borden Line, created by the federal government at the beginning of the 1960s; that Alberta sells its oil to the Americans much more cheaply than to Ontarians and Quebecers. Perhaps he might acknowledge that when there was almost no market for natural gas in the United States in 1983, the terrible Liberals in Ottawa extended the pipeline into Eastern Ontario and the largest part of Quebec to open up a new market for Albertan natural gas, all paid for by the federal government and not industry, as is generally the case.

Perhaps Quebec Premier François Legault made an error by talking about the "dirty oil" in Alberta, but oil is never clean. I don't know many people who wash their faces with this product in the morning. On the other hand, he showed himself to be very favourable to the construction of a pipeline that would bring natural gas from Alberta to the port of Chicoutimi and to the establishment of a large factory for the liquefication of gas, which would open up a new market for producers in the West.

As for me, who was a member of the federal cabinet for three decades and whose family on my mother's side arrived in Alberta in 1907 and now number four hundred Alberta members, I've always had a special interest in the province of my grandfather Boisvert. Also, in 2004, when I began to work with the large Calgary law firm Bennett Jones, on my first visit I was welcomed at our office by one of the greatest

Albertans I have known, the former Conservative premier of the province, Peter Lougheed. He reminded the journalists in attendance that on February 3, 1975, in the city of Winnipeg, the federal, Alberta, and Ontario governments finalized a trilateral agreement to enable the launch of the first extraction project at the Syncrude oil sands. He added that if I had not been present as the minister who was president of the Treasury Board, we would never have had an agreement.

I should perhaps add, for the edification of the ineffable Premier Kenney, that when he himself was a Conservative MP in Ottawa, I concluded an agreement with my friend the premier of Alberta Ralph Klein to offset the weakness of oil prices by agreeing that the federal government would authorize a deduction system for an accelerated amortization that would cost our treasury millions of dollars and decrease his fees. In 1996, this agreement between the Liberal prime minister in Ottawa and a Conservative minister in Edmonton revitalized the oil sands production in the region of Fort McMurray.

I could expound at length on this subject, discussing, for example, the referendum process and the conditions required by international law to gain independence, none of which presumably apply to Alberta. What would be the reaction of the federal parliamentarians who would have to vote on this issue, as is required by the 1999 Supreme Court decision, and the Clarity Act that Kenney himself supported in the Canadian Parliament as a federal member from Calgary?

Perhaps Mr. Kenney ought to follow the lead of Ralph Klein, who was premier of Alberta for ten years when I was prime minister of Canada, and with whom we were able to talk and to solve problems, without embarking on irresponsible and destructive demagogy. During the thirty years I was a minister and prime minister in Ottawa, I always had courteous relations with Peter Lougheed, Don Getty, and Ralph Klein, who stoutly and intelligently defended Alberta's interests and understood that the federal government too has its duties and responsibilities. I am proud of having been the only Liberal to have had Liberal members elected in Alberta during each of my elections since Louis St. Laurent in 1954. What is more, between 1993 and 2006, Alberta knew its longest period of prosperity, and that under a Liberal government in Ottawa. The difficult phase the province is weathering today began when two Calgary MPs, Prime Minister Stephen Harper and Jason Kenney, himself a minister, were in power in Ottawa.

I knew Jason Kenney as a young Conservative MP in the Opposition. He at certain times showed himself to be impossible, and at others, on the contrary, perfectly reasonable, even agreeable. When the euphoria of his victory wears off, I believe he'll want to become a Peter Lougheed or a Ralph Klein, at which time both Alberta and Canada would reap the benefits.

I wrote this chapter on August 5, 2019, and so before the elections in the course of which Alberta sent to Ottawa its MPs, all of whom are in the Opposition. In Calgary the following October 31, I found myself at a public meeting in front of six hundred people, along with none other than former Conservative prime minister Stephen Harper. When I had accepted the invitation in the spring, I had not realized that this meeting with Stephen Harper would be taking place only ten days after Canada's general election. Leaving Ottawa early that morning and during the four hours the flight lasted, I tormented myself with the thought that I had probably put myself in a bind by accepting this invitation. When I appeared before hundreds of Calgarians, I tipped them off right from the start that at the age of eighty-five, I had nothing to lose or gain from this exchange, and I told them frankly what I thought. I repeated all the points you've read in the preceding pages, and I asked Harper who had been the last federal prime minister to have altered the equalization formula. He admitted that it was himself, and that it was an error.

He explained his error by indicating that neighbouring Saskatchewan had become a province like Alberta, that is to say a rich province that was going to lose the federal money it had received for decades. And so he adjusted the formula to accommodate his prairie neighbour, but as a result, the only province not to receive equalization payments became Alberta. He also helped me to explain that the equalization money came out of the pockets of all Canadian taxpayers, so that an Alberta citizen does not pay more than one from Ontario or Quebec. And that if the province of Alberta did not qualify for these federal transfers, it's because Albertans do not pay a provincial sales tax, they pay less personal income tax than the citizens of other provinces, and it's the same for corporate taxes.

Our discussion, moderated by a competent journalist, unfolded cordially. I must say that I seasoned the facts with a dash of humour, and at no point was the audience rude to me. When it was all over, the two former prime ministers received a long standing ovation. The event was not made public because, for an unknown reason, there were no journalists present.

That same evening, Stephen Harper wrote on his Facebook page that he had been happy to meet with his friend, the twentieth prime minister of Canada, Jean Chrétien. As we say in Mauricie, *je l'avais échappé belle*, I had a narrow escape, but it proves that we shouldn't be afraid to tell the truth, and that the truth will have its way with the demagogy of Kenney and his neighbour Scott Moe, premier of Saskatchewan.

20

ON AIRPLANES

When Prime Minister Pierre Elliott Trudeau named me minister of Indian affairs and northern development, I never thought I would spend so much time in airplanes, or that I would have the adventures I'm going to describe. The minister who wants to do his work properly must visit Indigenous communities that are scattered over four hundred reserves or villages in all the Canadian provinces. He must also visit the national parks established in the four corners of the country. In addition, he is responsible for the northern territories, the Northwest Territories, the Yukon, and now the new territory of Nunavut. Going from Eastern Canada to the northwest, where the Yukon is situated, represents a distance farther than that from Halifax to London, England. I visited the Yukon four or five times a year, with two technical stops in Winnipeg and Edmonton to fill up on fuel. We had to factor in ten hours between the departure from Ottawa and the arrival in Whitehorse.

In 1969, on a flight out of Yellowknife, on the opposite side of the ten-passenger plane's centre aisle, the door suddenly flew open at a height of ten thousand feet. That was a shock and one hell of a fright for many on board! You should have seen the gentleman shaking, whose feet were just in front of the open door! One of the two pilots, the legendary Weldy Phipps, tall and sturdy, left his post to come to the back of the plane. He grabbed on tight to a seat back with his right hand, stuck half his body out of the cabin to grab the door handle with his left, and pulled it toward him, slamming the door and allaying our worst fears. And then he returned, nonchalant, to his seat in the cockpit, as if nothing had happened. There was an "ooph!" of relief from the passengers. We were able to go on with our trip in total calm, but I know that a number of us had taken the time to say our prayers.

On January 2, 1970, after having visited Coppermine, a small Inuit village in the north of the Northwest Territories, on the occasion of the centenary of those territories, I took the plane with my family to continue on to Holman, an island in the north of Inuvik. In January, the night lasts twenty-two hours, and after a rather turbulent ninety-minute flight, one of the pilots came to tell us that the winds were getting stronger and stronger, that our trip was encountering certain difficulties, and that we had to remain calm. I saw that he seemed very nervous himself and that his forehead was bathed in sweat. We seemed to be turning in circles, outside all was black, and we could see no lights on the ground.

After a great deal of turbulence, we were finally able to land. When we got out of the plane, the pilot told us that we had had a close call. He said that we had flown over the territory for a very long time because he couldn't see the landing field, which was swept by violent winds. Those winds made it impossible to light the oil lamps that served as landing guides. And there was no alternative, because the nearest village was a hundred kilometres away. The pilot informed me that it was an oblate missionary from Marie-Immaculée who had saved our lives. In fact, the whole village was awaiting this first visit from the minister responsible for the territories, and given the impossibility of lighting the oil lamps, Father Lapointe had had the idea of lining up snowmobiles on each side of the runway, with all their headlights lit. Without the presence of mind of this good Catholic priest, there's a fair chance that we would have ended our passage on Earth at Holman Island in the Northwest Territories, in the centenary year of that territory's founding. I never again saw this good Father Lapointe, but without him, I would probably never have become prime minister of Canada. Often, in my prayers, I thank this devoted missionary who could never have known on this January 2, 1970, that he had saved the life of a future Canadian prime minister along with his family.

One day, when I was travelling in a Beaver aircraft with big "balloon" tires near Norman Wells on the Mackenzie River, we were directed toward a drilling platform in the tundra. It was said that this old carrier could land just about anywhere, and the pilot came down as close as possible to the workers on the platform. After the visit, the pilot let us know that we had a problem, because the plane had very little room to take off, and we were at most two or three hundred feet from a swamp. Since we had to take off one way or another, we all had to sit at the rear of the plane, and he asked the most corpulent among us, who weighed 280 pounds, to sit in the tail and not in his seat.

When we were installed in the back of the plane, he started the engine, pushing down hard on the brakes. We heard the engine vibrating more and more strongly; suddenly, he let go of the brakes, and after a short distance, the plane took off. We had all listened to the pilot, and no one seemed nervous. It was only after we found ourselves at dinner that we all realized what luck we'd had. For the six years and four months that I was minister of native affairs and northern development, I flew very often with these bush pilots, whom I always found competent, sure of themselves, and debonair, risking their lives every day. I salute them with the greatest possible respect.

During an official visit to Iran in 1976, I had some exchanges with the shah of Iran, in the course of which we discussed the individual freedoms that were being flouted in his country. As minister of industry, trade, and commerce, I was in that respect deviating from the subject of my visit, but I have to admit that the shah was always very courteous and showed no reluctance to broach the subject. After a rather heated discussion, he told me, in impeccable French, "Many of you hope for my departure, but whoever replaces me will be even less acceptable, and the Western world will miss me." I must say that he was right up to a point, when we think about Ayatollah Khomeini's Iran.

After my visit to the shah and his prime minister, Amir Abbas Hoveyda, my delegation, Aline, and I took the Canadian government's JetStar to travel farther north on the Caspian Sea and to visit a paper mill being built by a Canadian company. After a short time in the air, the pilot announced that the plane was having a problem, and that we had to go back to the Tehran airport. As we were circling to burn off fuel, we could see ambulances and fire trucks waiting for us. As a reception committee, they were not very reassuring.

We finally set down at a much higher speed than usual, with the distinct impression that the runway would not be long enough for us to be able to stop. Fortunately, it all ended well, without any involvement of the rescue services. This unusual landing was made necessary by the bursting of the tire at the front of the plane, which had in turn broken the braking flaps on the aircraft's wings. After our departure, the airport workers had spotted the rubber on the runway and had alerted the pilot. What would have happened if the rubber had ended up outside the runway and had not been noticed?

———

At the beginning of the 1970s, when I was minister of Indian affairs and northern development, I travelled one Sunday morning from Montreal to Toronto. I was alone in Air Canada business class, and I was calmly reading a newspaper, when I heard the pilot addressing the passengers. I was paying no attention to what he was saying, but suddenly a flight attendant burst into the cabin and sat on the other side of the aisle, trembling like a leaf and bathed in tears. Abruptly, the plane swerved to the left and plunged toward the ground, which was looming up at terrifying speed. I thought about Aline and the children, and I offered my life to the Lord, certain that I was going to die. At a few hundred feet from the ground, the pilot righted the plane, which landed abruptly and rapidly came to a stop.

An emergency exit opened in the rear, toward which everyone converged; some were shouting, others weeping, and I noticed a panicked young woman with two small children. I picked up the two children like two footballs, one under my left arm and the other under my right, and with everyone else I ran toward the emergency exit. After finding myself on the runway, I returned the children to their mother and asked one of the pilots the reason for such a dramatic landing. He told me that it was a bomb alert. That was what the pilot had told the passengers before performing his aeronautic manoeuvre. Now I understood the panic that had overtaken the passengers. Had I listened to the pilot's announcement regarding a possible bomb, I would have been able to calm the flight attendant and the mother of the young children, because as minister of Native affairs and northern development, I'd had to evacuate my office for bomb alerts on several occasions, and I'd come to the conclusion that this was the best technique for someone who just wants to sow panic, because anyone who really plants a bomb always wants it to explode. My past experiences had taught me not to lose my cool under such circumstances.

After a visit to Sweden in the summer of 2001, I left Stockholm for the Azores, because I'd promised Portuguese Canadians to one day visit this territory from which had come a large number of immigrants. In fact, I'd had the pleasure of meeting many of them in the nation's capital. Soon after departure, the Challenger aircraft began to behave bizarrely, and its nose tilted downward. The oxygen masks dropped, and the pilot ordered us to place them over our mouths. Then the pilot asked the only three passengers, my bodyguard Pierre Giguère, my assistant Bruce Hartley, and me if we preferred to land in Oslo, in Norway, or to go back to Stockholm, where the rest of the delegation was waiting to return to Ottawa on board a Canadian Army Airbus. We returned to Sweden, and the visit to the Azores was cancelled. We rejoined the rest of the delegation, and a half-hour later, we were in an Airbus on the way to Canada.

As we were flying blithely over the Atlantic, the pilot came to inform Pierre, Bruce, and me that we had to move about as little as possible, because after the abrupt descent of the plane and the decompression with its "bends" effect, airline rules did not allow us to take another plane until seventy-two hours had passed.

The Defence Department authorities had only realized the error after our departure from Sweden in the military Airbus. The chief doctor of the Canadian Armed Forces had himself spoken to the pilots and had instructed them to tell us that we had to move as little as possible during the rest of the trip. He had also told them to choose Quebec City as this Atlantic crossing's destination.

As there had been an error in communication between the plane and the general headquarters in Ottawa, the authorities thought that thirty people had been exposed to decompression, and at Jean Lesage Airport in Quebec City a bus and a number of ambulances were waiting for us. But in fact, only three of us had experienced the swift descent of a plane—an error, these things happen. Three doctors were waiting anxiously to examine us at the airport. After the tests, one of them informed Pierre Giguère and myself that we had suffered no damage. I joked, "That's only to be expected; Shawinigan guys are tough." Giguère and I are from the same hometown.

And so we left Quebec City for Shawinigan, and as we had slept well on the plane and had time to kill, Bruce and I went to play golf. I don't know if it was thanks to the bends, but that afternoon, for the first and last time in my life, I scored a seventy-nine. Not only that, but Bruce too played the best game of his life! Perhaps I ought to tip off the great pro players we see on TV that a brutal descent in a plane and a bit of the bends will improve the quality of your play in spectacular fashion, as it did for Bruce and myself. Who knows?

21

DECENTRALIZATION

When I became president of the Treasury Board in 1974, the federal government had decided that we needed a decentralization program, because compared to other countries, the Canadian government had too many civil servants in the national capital. At the time, it was thought that it would be good for the economy to scatter the federal bureaucrats across all of Canada's regions, and as president of the Treasury Board, I was the most appropriate minister to be in charge of the dossier.

This was no small task, because for many civil servants, the idea of leaving Ottawa to be spread all around the country was not a pleasing prospect. It was worse for the senior officials, who feared that a possible transfer to other regions would distance them from the decision-making and be an obstacle to their gaining a coveted promotion that would advance their careers. The idea of losing jobs was infuriating for MPs elected in the national capital regions, and they did all they could to halt the project. Being the minister responsible for this whole operation was not going to make my life easy on Parliament Hill.

Choosing who would be leaving and where the new offices would be set up was a very complex task. What was most difficult was coming up with objective criteria that would justify before the House of Commons and the Senate the decision taken by the member ministers on the Treasury Board. The speed of execution was soon shown to be a crucial element in the unfolding of the operation, and so we planned the relocation of thousands of jobs throughout seven provinces and more than twenty cities in less than twelve months. You have to realize that during this period, my cage was being rattled in the national capital region by MPs, bureaucrats, unions, the local press, and even my parliamentary secretary, who finally quit in a huff. I was sure that people in the Ottawa region were going to resent me for a long time, but that was not the case, and sixteen years later when I became leader of the Liberal Party and prime minister of Canada, elected and re-elected in 1993, 1997, and 2000, we won each time in every one of the national capital's ridings.

On October 24, 2019, I went to Shawinigan to celebrate the fortieth anniversary of the opening of the tax data centre, which now employs 1,800 people. In thanking me, someone in the crowd, who had made his whole career in the city where he was born, asked me how I had been able to give my hometown that advantage without being accused of political patronage.

I replied that as an MP, it was my duty to try to obtain something important for my region. Because the tax data centre required a large number of part-time employees, the Ottawa region had problems filling these posts. That is why we decided to establish regional centres: two in Ontario, two in Quebec, one in Atlantic Canada, one in the Prairies, and one in British Columbia. In Quebec, Montreal already being a big city and Quebec City being the capital of the province, neither one represented a reasonable decentralization. As we wanted to have a tax data centre in the middle of Quebec, two regions qualified: Sherbrooke and Mauricie. Since Mauricie was more populous than Sherbrooke, it was chosen.

An additional consideration was that the town of Shawinigan had suffered a loss of three thousand jobs over the course of the preceding fifteen years, as electrochemistry was replaced by petrochemistry. The criteria for economic difficulty favoured my native town. I knew that I would have to provide explanations, because I assumed that a decentralization that favoured my electoral riding would be harshly criticized. I managed it by showing that, because the geographical centre of Mauricie between Louiseville and Saint-Tite was Shawinigan-South, it was logical to install the centre there, because hundreds of employees, mainly women, would be at a reasonable distance from their place of work. This time, geography came to my aid.

Among the harder decisions I had to take, the most complex was moving the Department of Veterans Affairs. When I told the ministers on the Treasury Board that we had to envisage transferring that department, the minister responsible was Dan MacDonald, a member from Prince Edward Island, himself a veteran who had lost an arm and a leg in the war. When he returned to civilian life, he became a successful farmer and a very popular politician, despite the enormous handicap he had inherited from his service to the nation. He was the oldest member of the cabinet, likeable and funny. He never raised his voice and had only friends on Parliament Hill.

As soon as I brought up the possibility of transferring the department he ran, I saw him lose his cool for the very first time, raise his voice, and tell me that he objected, that he would never accept it, and we'd have to walk over his body before this stupid idea would go forward. I then took the floor and said to Dan, "Don't get mad; if that's the way it is, I'll withdraw my suggestion. I don't want you angry with me, but it's too bad for the citizens of Prince Edward Island, because I envisaged transferring hundreds of jobs to the beautiful city of Charlottetown!" You should have seen his face! I'd chosen Charlottetown because I knew that only Dan MacDonald would be able to carry out the project without there being a huge fuss made by the veterans and unions. The transference of the department was accomplished forty years ago, and every time I've gone to Prince Edward Island since, I've asked to pass in front of the Veterans Affairs building, which bears the name of this war hero, farmer, and politician adored by his constituents, this true gentleman: Daniel J. Macdonald.

When you become an MP, you're told that you've been elected to help, through your work, to better the lives of your constituents. Now very often, the voters and journalists find that you've not done enough for your fellow citizens. But when the MP succeeds, especially if he's a minister, then it becomes "patronage." I had to face such accusations when I managed to establish a national park in Mauricie. As minister of Indian affairs and northern development, I was responsible for Parks Canada, historical sites and monuments, and the Canadian Wildlife Service.

While I was defending the cost estimates for my department before a House of Commons committee, I was accused of "patronage" for developing a national park in my riding. When I took the floor to reply to the accusation, I pretended to be caught in the trap. I gestured nervously, groped for words, pretended to be contrite. I said that I was troubled to have to admit that, in fact, the Mauricie national park was not really in my riding, but rather in that of Berthier-Maskinongé-Lanaudière, represented by a Conservative, and also in that of Champlain, whose member was in the Social Credit Party, which forced me to reveal to my constituents in Saint-Maurice that only 5 per cent of the national park's area was in their electoral riding.

But there were, in fact, only two entrances to the park's territory: one was situated at Saint-Mathieu-du-Parc, and the other at Saint-Jean-des-Piles, two villages that are in my riding. The two opposition members didn't know that the park was part of their ridings, because there was no road to access it. The part of the park in the two neighbouring ridings is made up of vast spaces, which are wild Crown land. The people of Shawinigan who read this text will be very surprised to learn that the largest part of La Mauricie National Park is not in Saint-Maurice. Thus, no one can accuse me of favouritism, even if the economic benefits of the park's creation have been largely bestowed on the citizens and businesspeople of my riding.

22

A HUNDRED YEARS AGO

On Friday, November 6, 2019, I went to Montreal to celebrate Pierre Elliott Trudeau's centenary. He was born on October 18, 1919. The event took place a few days after his birth date, because at that point almost all the guests were busy working toward—who would have guessed it?—the re-election of the Liberal prime minister, his son Justin.

What emotion and what a pleasure to find oneself in the magnificent art deco house built, and for a time occupied by, the celebrated architect Ernest Cormier, and acquired by Pierre upon his retirement in 1984, after having served nineteen years as an MP and minister, and fifteen years as our prime minister.

His son Alexandre, whom I have all my life called Sacha, had invited one hundred people to the reception, where I had the pleasure of again seeing Margaret Trudeau, Justin and Sacha's mother, and the surprise of meeting Pierre Elliott's six grandchildren, all very cute, well behaved, and clearly in good form physically, which would have pleased their grandfather.

On April 4, 1967, Lester B. Pearson invited me into the cabinet during a reshuffling that affected only three MPs: Pierre Elliott Trudeau became minister of justice and attorney general of Canada, John Turner inherited the post of registrar general, and I was named minister of state for finance. It was called at the time "minister without portfolio," but for a young man of thirty-three it was more than acceptable, especially if one considers that the average age of the cabinet members was fifty-one at that time. A rare phenomenon, all three being sworn in would later become prime ministers of Canada. Hats off to Lester B. Pearson's judgment and intuition!

Alexandre, who was master of ceremonies, talked with great feeling about his life with his father, expressing himself with love and objectivity, thoughtfully, as one would have hoped, and after he spoke he yielded the floor to his brother, Justin. That was a special moment for me, because for years I had sat to the left of Trudeau the father in the House of Commons and the cabinet. When there were pauses in the proceedings, Pierre and I sometimes talked about his sons, Justin, Sacha, and Michel.

Listening to Justin the prime minister talk solemnly and with admiration about his father, I thought to myself that Pierre Trudeau, my boss and friend for fifteen years, would have been very proud of him, while most likely keeping his peace on the subject. He was a very reserved man, who kept his emotions to himself. After Prime Minister Justin's excellent presentation, Alexandre asked the young people of his age, almost all associated with the Pierre Elliott Trudeau Foundation, to voice their feelings on the occasion of this historic centenary. They all mirrored today's Canada, representing a variety of colours, religions, and languages, and expressing themselves with elegance in our two official languages. I was there with a number of companions in arms of the Trudeau era, including my friend Marc Lalonde, who was Pierre's principal secretary, a seasoned minister in his cabinet, and an intimate of his.

None of these young speakers had been born when we were talking then of a social revolution that began with Mike Pearson and was pursued with zeal under Pierre Elliott, aiming to modernize our country by grappling with difficult issues: the death penalty, divorce, homosexuality, official languages, refugees, the repatriation of the constitution, and above all the Canadian Charter of Rights and Freedoms. For me, it is an immense source of pride to have participated in governments that have been key to this progress, especially the Charter of Rights, to which all those who spoke made reference.

When Alexandre asked me to take the floor, I was happy to pay homage to a great prime minister, one who significantly raised Canada's international profile. I was able to tell the children, grandchildren, and Margaret Trudeau that they all had reason to be proud of Pierre Elliott Trudeau, because he was a great man in all facets of his life.

As practically everyone had referred to the Charter of Rights, I thought I would describe how I became minister of justice, responsible for developing and passing through Parliament this most important legislative project of Pierre's political career. The nomination was a bit complicated, but here is how it happened.

In 1979, to everyone's surprise, Joe Clark's Conservatives won the general election against Pierre Trudeau's Liberals. In the preceding government, I had been president of the Treasury Board and finance minister, which had merited me the nickname "Doctor No." It goes without saying that many in the party blamed me for the defeat, and I knew that a lot of pressure was being exerted to ensure that I would not again be named finance minister.

After only seven months in power, the Clark government lost a vote of confidence in the House, which automatically triggered a general election that the Liberals won with a Pierre Elliott Trudeau at their helm who had reneged on his initial idea of resigning. After the election, and before the formation of the ministerial team, I met with Allan MacEachen, a member of Trudeau's most recent government, as minister of foreign affairs and senior minister in the cabinet. He informed me that Trudeau had summoned him to discuss the cabinet's makeup, and that he wanted to serve as finance minister because after having been an economics professor at St. Francis Xavier University in Nova Scotia, he'd always dreamed of being responsible for state finances. I told him that I understood his desire and that of his friends, but I thought that, as I knew him, he would not be very happy at Finance. He asked me if I would like to take his place at Foreign Affairs.

The following days were rather complicated, and when I met Pierre Trudeau, he confirmed that MacEachen had recommended offering me foreign affairs. I told him that I would accept the job with pleasure. It was then that he dropped the bomb, confessing that he wanted to put me in charge of the referendum that would soon be held in Quebec, and that I ought to accept the post of minister of justice. I replied that I did not want to be responsible for the referendum. He responded that the referendum, the repatriation of the Constitution, and the Charter of Rights were his priorities. He added this potent argument: "The house is burning in Quebec and you want to be in Washington, London, Paris, Moscow, and Tokyo . . ." I answered, laughing, "Pierre, tell me what a big brother would advise his little brother!" He picked up the thread: "The big brother is going to name his little brother minister of justice, attorney general of Canada, minister responsible for the referendum, the repatriation of the Constitution, and the Charter of Rights, and minister of state for social programs. So the little brother can't say that the big brother doesn't have confidence in him." I ended the conversation, once more on a light note, saying, "As the house is burning in Quebec, hand me the garden hose!" And I entered into the hardest years of my long political career.

Once the law on the repatriation of the Constitution had passed the stage of long negotiations with the committees of the House of Commons and the Senate, my prime minister charged me with ensuring that the British Parliament would at last pass a law putting an end to the humiliating obligation of asking the British to amend our Constitution. I went to London to push things forward, but I found that there were still those who were nostalgic for the Empire and wanted to tell us what to do, which led me to participate in some bizarre conversations.

When I arrived in London, I was told that the House of Lords was going to vote on the bill that very evening. With my friend Alastair Gillespie, former minister of industry, trade, and commerce, I went to witness the last vote the British Parliament would pass concerning the former Dominion. Once the vote was over, Alastair Gillespie, an anglophone born in British Columbia, and former federal minister elected in Ontario, and Jean Chrétien, a francophone born in rural Quebec, and minister of justice, went out to celebrate this historic moment in a real English pub.

The next morning, I went to Buckingham Palace to inform the Queen of the vote concerning the most recent law dealing with Canada and decreeing that the Parliament of Great Britain had now cut the final juridical tie that linked it to its former colony. As well, I was to tell Her Majesty that Prime Minister Trudeau was inviting her to come to Ottawa to sign the royal proclamation. Since 1967, I had met her on several occasions, including on a four-day trip marking the centenary of the Northwest Territories, and she often employed the French language to talk to me. And so I asked her if I could express myself in the language of Molière, and she graciously accepted. At the moment of cutting the last juridical link with Great Britain, and having contributed to giving Canada its two official languages, I found it symbolically significant that the last official proclamation to the Queen concerning this historic event take place in London, at Buckingham Palace, in my native tongue, French.

Sometimes, when I talk of the Queen, I say in jest, "Do you know why, when I meet Her Majesty, the conversation takes place in French? It's because she can't stand my English!"

When the Queen came to Ottawa to sign the royal proclamation, protocol decreed that she would sign first, followed by the prime minister of Canada, the secretary of state, and the registrar general. Trudeau wanted me to sign the parchment because I'd done the work, and so he ordered that my name be inscribed on the proclamation just under that of the Queen, at the top of the document, while he, Secretary of State Gerald Regan, and Registrar General André Ouellet would sign in the lower part of the document.

On April 17, 1982, the day of the proclamation on Parliament Hill, the Queen signed first, the prime minister followed, and I was the third to add my name to this historic document. When I took the pen that Trudeau had just used, I realized that he had broken the point and that it was no longer working. And so I let a word escape my mouth, and on the video of the event's coverage, you can see Her Majesty looking left and right to see if others had heard, before bursting out laughing. I finally took the other pen sitting on the table, and I added my signature to the famous document. For years, journalists and other citizens have asked me what I said to make the Queen laugh on such a solemn occasion. I replied, "I can't tell you; it's a state secret." I had in fact furtively let slip the "word of Cambronne," *mer*——. The bilingual Queen's fine ear caught it, and she had a good laugh.

23

JULY 2019, MY SUMMER *HORRIBILIS*

It's August 1, 2019, and I'm picking up my pen again after more than a month. I'd arrived at my house on Lac des Piles on June 12 to spend a summer doing little work and relaxing. But my plans changed in a very unexpected way. On June 28, I had to have surgery on my left leg, and I was forbidden to swim or play golf, two of my favourite leisure activities, for two weeks. A fine beginning . . .

I'd agreed to make one trip during the summer, and I arrived in Hong Kong on July 8. No sooner did I land than I had an attack of kidney stones. So having just visited Quebec City for treatment to my leg, here I was back in the hospital in great pain, this time in Hong Kong, where the doctors told me that they could do nothing for five days because I had to temporarily stop taking the anticoagulants that prevent blood clots from forming in my heart.

I was one of the main guests invited to a big conference organized by Tung Chee-hwa, who ran the former British colony for close to eight years after its return to China. He had to tell the press that I was hospitalized in Asia, and that it was an emergency. So I found myself in news bulletins circulated by Bloomberg. Because some people assumed I was dying, I had to staunch the fire as soon as possible. By Wednesday morning, the medicine had eased my pain, and taking advantage of this moment of respite, I made my way to the convention. To everyone's surprise, my friend Tung offered to have me make my presentation. When I got to the microphone, the pain suddenly vanished, to be replaced by the adrenalin that always has a surprising effect on the old fighter that I am.

As those attending the conference were American and Chinese businesspeople and bureaucrats, I told them that Canada was the ham in the middle of the American and Chinese sandwich because of Meng Wanzhou, who was awaiting trial concerning her extradition to the United States. I explained to them that we ought not always to be pessimistic, because if we look back, the world has made great progress in reducing famine, infant mortality, poverty, and so on. The gravest problem is in the lamentable sharing of wealth. I went on to explain that dialogue between the various parties was essential, and that even if there were persisting differences, it was possible to solve certain problems.

Because Neil Bush, brother of former U.S. president George W. Bush, was attending the conference, I gave the example that despite my refusing to allow Canada to participate in the Iraq war, I continued to have good personal relations with the United States to the end of my mandate in December 2003. The speaker who followed me to the podium was Goh Chok Tong, who had been prime minister of Singapore for thirteen years. He explained to the audience that, like me, he had been pressured to involve his country in the coalition favouring the Iraq war, and after studying the Americans' argument justifying the invasion of Saddam Hussein's country, he too became skeptical as to the justification for military intervention. But as his country sold a lot of arms to the United States, he'd decided to include his country in the military coalition. Today, he regretted having been too "pragmatic" and not having followed the dictates of his conscience. He congratulated Canada and its prime minister for having had the courage to say no to the United States.

Given the severity of my pain, I had to leave the conference prematurely, but the doctors had told me that, in any case, they could not operate to crush the rather large stone interfering with the functioning of my right kidney before Friday, when the prescribed delay following the suspension of my anticoagulant medication would be over. So I still had a three-day wait in Hong Kong. At the end of the conference, I was scheduled to travel, on Wednesday, to Hanoi, the capital of Vietnam, to discuss with the prime minister an important decision concerning Canadian businesses. I thought, "To suffer here or three hours away by plane, in another hotel, it's the same thing." So at the end of the day, I took the plane to Hanoi. After a sleepless night, I went to meet Nguyen Xuan Phuc, the prime minister of Vietnam, a country whose economic progress is outstripping that of all its neighbours. After a very fruitful meeting, the prime minister invited me to meet the press to explain the nature of our discussions and their results. As in the good old days, I faced up to the journalists.

Once my work was finished, I made my way to the Hanoi airport to fly back to Hong Kong. It was Thursday night, and I went directly to the hospital, where, knocked out by drugs, I finally had a good night's sleep. On waking, I immediately went under the knife and was treated to the new techniques that consisted of fragmenting the stone lodged in my right kidney. Even if the crushing of this unfortunate stone was a success, not everything was reduced to dust, and I continued to suffer, if less intensely.

One of the recommendations made in order to recover as quickly as possible was to drink a lot of water to flush out what was left of the stone. Which is what I did, faithfully, for the rest of the day and the next, until my departure for Toronto. But fifteen hours in a plane while drinking plenty of water to drown my stone was something of a feat, and I got no sleep. Fifteen hours in such a state is a long time. So: arrival in Toronto, connection to Montreal, then two hours in a car to Lac des Piles in Mauricie guaranteed that this trip, prolonged by twelve hours since we were coming from the west, would be burned into my memory for a long time.

Following the advice of the Chinese doctors, I went, on my return, to the Sainte-Marie hospital in Trois-Rivières and followed up with a urologist, who helped me greatly during the days when my kidney continued to empty itself of pulverized particles from the notorious stone that had been intent on making me suffer.

At about eight o'clock on Friday, August 2, my neighbour and friend Dr. Normand Ayotte, phoned me to inquire about my state and offer some encouragement. I assured him that everything was going better. As it was very hot and I was not sleeping, I went out on my veranda around midnight to contemplate a sky glittering with stars and to take advantage of the Maurician countryside's fresh air. The lake water was reflecting the moonlight, and it suddenly tempted me. Why not cool off in the pure water of Lac des Piles? In my dressing gown and without shoes, I went down toward the lake, moving off the stone staircase to make it easier on my feet. I'd decided to walk on the lawn, which descends rather abruptly, without realizing that the night's dew, at one o'clock in the morning, makes the grass as slippery as a skating rink.

And so here is Chrétien, flat on his back, his left arm fractured after connecting with a stone! I rolled to the bottom of the hill, where, in pain, I cried out, "Help!" Obviously, at that hour, no one heard me, and it took me forty-five minutes to crawl back up to the house, unable to stand up. My cries finally woke our employee, who found me in agony, stretched out almost naked on the stones. She called an ambulance and Dr. Ayotte, whom I'd told barely five hours earlier that I was finally getting better. And oops! Here I was at two in the morning in the Shawinigan hospital.

After the X-rays, the charming orthopaedist told me that the fracture was too near the shoulder for her to apply a cast. So I had to keep my arm in a sling until mid-September. For eighty years, I'd been coming to spend my vacation beside this famous lake, one of the most beautiful in the Laurentians, and for the first time I couldn't swim in its clear and refreshing water—what a drag!

And so my 2019 summer was one of doctors and hospitals in Quebec City, Hong Kong, Trois-Rivières, and Shawinigan. Not what I would have hoped for, but what can you do?

My host in Hong Kong, Tung Chee-hwa, had certainly chosen a first-class hospital, and my stay there was perfect. Back in Quebec, the hospitals, the personnel, the doctors, and the services were perhaps not as exceptional as in the finest hospital in the richest city of Asia, but they certainly had nothing to be ashamed of. On the contrary, I was pleasantly surprised.

But where there was an enormous difference was at the moment of my departure. Everywhere, I simply congratulated the personnel and thanked them sincerely for the good care they gave me. On the other hand, in Asia's richest city, you have to present your credit card on the way out. After that, I was fortunately not in the mood for a shopping spree, because I don't think the sum left to me would have allowed for many extravagances! Long live Canada's system of equal health care for all, without billing.

24

A PM NOT LIKE THE OTHERS

A few years ago, the University of Toronto Press decided to reprint the memoirs of the University of Toronto's most celebrated graduate and asked me to write the foreword for the three books constituting the memoirs of the Right Honourable Lester B. Pearson. These are very interesting writings, enabling us to follow the career of one of the great public servants in the Ottawa bureaucracy. A high-level diplomat, he was second in command at the High Commission of Canada in the United Kingdom during the crucial period of World War II. Later, he participated in the founding of the United Nations. Reluctantly, he left his diplomatic career to become foreign affairs minister in the government of Louis St. Laurent. In 1957, for his efforts in defusing the Suez Canal crisis, he was awarded the Nobel Peace Prize. And in 1963, he became a superb prime minister for our country. And so I am sharing with you what I wrote on the subject of this exceptional person.

FOREWORD TO THE 2015 EDITION
THE RT. HON. JEAN CHRÉTIEN

On 8 April 1963, Lester Pearson became prime minister of Canada and I was elected to the House of Commons for the first time. Mr. Pearson was sixty-six years old, the son of a Methodist minister from Ontario, and a Nobel Peace Prize winner. He had lived in grand embassies and dined with Churchill, Roosevelt, and de Gaulle. I was twenty-nine, the son of a factory machinist from French-speaking, Roman Catholic Quebec, and a small-town lawyer. Our worlds were completely different and I never imagined he would be the kind of guy I'd go fishing with. From the first day I met him, however, the distance between us quickly evaporated.

I always joked that I came to Mr. Pearson's attention because of his love of baseball. One day he asked me if I would pitch in the annual softball game that used to take place between politicians and the press corps. Though I had never been much of a sports star, I did well enough, and to our coach's delight, we won. Not long afterwards he made me his parliamentary secretary!

Parliamentary secretaries don't have any formal or legal role, they're just there to be of help in any way that they're asked. However, in those days the post was usually a sign that you were considered to be ministerial material and on your way to the Cabinet. But two developments almost blocked me.

The first happened in 1964 when I was asked to consider returning to Quebec to run for the provincial Liberals in a by-election in Shawinigan. I was tempted. It was the early days of the Quiet Revolution, Quebec City was an exciting place to be, and Premier Jean Lesage himself told me that he needed someone of my youth and experience on his team, which was as close as he could come to guaranteeing me a position in his government.

When rumours reached Ottawa, Mr. Pearson called me into his office and asked me if they were true. "Yes," I replied, "I'm thinking of going."

Those were difficult days for him. He was trying to help French Canadians across Canada and combat the incipient separatist movement in Quebec, but he was in a minority situation, the Conservatives were imped-ing a lot of his initiatives (including the introduction of a Canadian flag and official bilingualism), and there were a spate of scandals involving his Quebec minis-ters. "Jean," he asked, "do you believe in Canada?"

"Of course I believe in Canada," I said, somewhat taken aback. "If you wish, I will not go, Prime Minister."

"No, don't make that decision right away," he said. "Go home and take a week to think about it."

I went back to Shawinigan and consulted with my wife, Aline, and nineteen of my friends. Seventeen advised me to go to Quebec City, because all the activities that mat-tered locally—schools, hospitals, welfare—were provincial responsibilities. That was my own inclination, I must admit. But Aline and two of my closest advisers, Fernand D. Lavergne and Marcel Crête, convinced me otherwise. Though Mr. Pearson didn't promise me anything, he was obviously grateful.

By 1965 I was often mentioned favourably in the Quebec press as an active, "new guard" Liberal and my name kept showing up in their short lists of potential Cabinet ministers. But a second obstacle presented itself when Mr. Pearson decided—against my advice, I might add—to call an early election in the hope of securing a majority government.

At one point I was out campaigning with him in his riding, Algoma East, when he told me of a new development. The Liberals had recruited three exceptional candidates in Quebec: the well-known union leader Jean Marchand, the distinguished journalist Gérard Pelletier, and a law professor with a radical reputation named Pierre Elliott Trudeau. "What do you think of them coming with us?" Mr. Pearson asked me.

I thought it was a good idea and would help rebuild the party in Quebec. "But I have a problem with this guy Trudeau," I added. "We'll never get him elected anywhere."

"You know, Jean," Mr. Pearson added, "this might mean that you won't come into the Cabinet as quickly as hoped."

I understood his situation. "Prime Minister," I said, "if you have better people than me, you should promote them before me."

After the election, which produced another minority, he made Marchand a minister right away, but he surprised everyone by bypassing Pelletier, Trudeau, and myself and appointing Jean-Pierre Côté, an older, likeable MP with powerful supporters in Cabinet.

I was standing near the Prime Minister's office when Mr. Pearson spotted me and called me in. "Jean," he said, "you're mad at me because I named Côté a minister instead of you."

"I cannot be mad at you, Mr. Pearson," I said, though of course I was very disappointed, "because I'm not in a position to question your judgment." Besides, he could disarm anyone with a pat on the back and his warm charm.

"Someday you will understand, Jean," he said. "I'm going to appoint you parliamentary secretary to Mitchell Sharp in Finance. You will learn things there, and I hope you will become the first French-Canadian Minister of Finance. If I had taken you into the Cabinet today, in the traditional French-Canadian portfolio of Postmaster General that I've given to Côté, it might not lead you to greater things."

Though I can't be sure if his words were merely kindness, they turned out to be prophetic. He subsequently told me how struck he had been that, when all the Liberal MPs, English- or French-speaking, were asked to indicate which committees they wanted to join, I was the only one who had ticked the Finance and Banking Committee as my first choice.

Mr. Pearson must have received good reports of my work from Mitchell Sharp, for he summoned me to his office one morning in 1967 and gave me good news. On April 4 I was sworn in as Minister without Portfolio attached to Finance, along with two other future prime ministers: John Turner and Pierre Elliott Trudeau. In January 1968 he elevated me to Minister of National Revenue.

The Pearson government may have looked chaotic, but it wasn't a case of weak management or lack of direction. He was very, very tough in controlling his ministers, and he knew what had to be tackled. Contrary to the public impression, Mr. Pearson was much less consensual than Mr. Trudeau. There would be great storms during the Cabinet meetings, with ministers pounding the table and raging at each other. Eventually the Prime Minister would say, "It's time to go to lunch, so I'll take care of the matter." He had his own views and, for the most part, he just did what he wanted to do.

Though not every minister was strong, history has confirmed the strength of people such as Mitchell Sharp, Walter Gordon, Allan MacEachen, Paul Martin Sr., Lionel Chévrier, and Guy Favreau. They were full of experience and ideas, and though that sometimes made for a fractious and leaky group, with plenty of their ideological and political battles showing up in the press the next day, they normally rallied around Mr. Pearson whenever he was in trouble. His diplomatic skills allowed him to perform calmly when trapped in a crisis, and his cheery awkwardness made everyone want to come to his rescue. People felt warm towards him, they respected his values and his humanity, and we all thought he was a great man.

It was a tumultuous era, and the problems that overtook him were controversial, often emotional ones. There were also the normal difficulties of minority governments, compounded by a Leader of the Opposition who was highly irresponsible. John Diefenbaker always seemed in an angry mood—as though Mr. Pearson had interrupted his God-given destiny to be prime minister—and he exploited the bad luck of some Liberal ministers by exaggerating their so-called scandals.

Lester Pearson shaped my vision of what Canada could and should be, both at home and on the world stage. He once said to me, "The biggest mistake ever made in Canada was when Queen Victoria chose Ottawa over Montreal as the national capital. It was a bad move because Ottawa was an English city." And he was determined to right that wrong. He began the effort to make the capital the lively, bilingual centre it is today and to ensure that federal services became available in both official languages.

Mr. Pearson loved Canada, and he loved it passionately. He knew from his rich international career that a democratic and liberal country's true worth is measured by how tolerantly it treats its minorities and how generously it shares its wealth. He set up the Royal Commission on Bilingualism and Biculturalism and the Royal Commission on the Status of Women. He fought tooth and nail, and with great personal bravery, for a distinctive Canadian flag. He introduced the Canada Student Loan Plan that made a university education possible for so many more Canadians. He sought to make the Canadian immigration process blind to race and religion. He brought in the Canada Pension Plan and Medicare over the objections of the entrenched interests.

Like all Canadians, each in their own way, I owe Mr. Pearson a tremendous debt of gratitude. He profoundly changed our lives and our country for the better. Canada is the best! *Vive le Canada!*

25

ABC 2000

Today is Tuesday, February 4, 2020. It's ten thirty in the morning, I'm watching the news, and in the United States, in the state of Iowa, they have not yet been able to compile the results for yesterday evening's 1,100 caucuses, while hundreds of millions of people in the United States, Canada, Mexico, and everywhere in the world, are riveted to their television sets to find out who won the tight delegate race for the Democratic convention taking place in a few months. What a humiliation for American technology, reputed to be the best in the world. And what a delight for the Republicans, who will not hesitate to mock the Democrats, saying, "How can we entrust the most important presidency in the world to a political party that cannot even organize a popular consultation in a state whose population is barely more than 300,000?"

This all reminds me of the presidential election in the autumn of 2000, when the Democratic candidate was Al Gore, and the Republican candidate George W. Bush. The vote took place on Tuesday, November 7, and it took five weeks after the sealing of the ballot boxes before the identity of the new president was at last revealed. Five chaotic weeks with a mishmash of recounts, broken machines, administrative errors, legal proceedings, and appeals to higher courts and ultimately the Supreme Court. Meanwhile, in Canada, a Federal election took place on November 27, three weeks after that of the United States. A few days prior to the election, the American television network ABC dispatched a journalist to see how Canadians were going to proceed in their vote counting and avoid a disaster similar to that in Florida.

We had changed the voting hours, so that the voters in the east would cast their ballots an hour later and those in British Columbia an hour earlier than in previous elections, making the disparity between the Halifax vote and that of Vancouver only one hour. Also, instead of having complicated machines that sometimes do not function all that well, in Canada we used the old-fashioned procedure of a paper ballot on which, with a pencil, one inscribes an X in front of the chosen candidate's name. After the polls close, the candidates' representatives are present when the state's official agents open the ballot boxes. Every ballot is counted, one by one, by hand, an operation that generally takes half an hour, and in two hours at the most, all the votes from the east to the west of the country are computed and made public.

The American journalist was extremely impressed by the simplicity, the ease, the logic, and the effectiveness of our voting system.

While fifteen days after voting day in the United States, the Americans still did not know whether Gore or Bush had won, and would not for another three long weeks, the ABC journalist concluded that Canadians would know their winner's name an hour after the polls closed. The American commentator concluded his report, saying, "Here in the United States, we still do not know, after two weeks, who will be president, while in Canada, the vote will have taken place in one week, and everyone is already certain that Jean Chrétien will be elected prime minister for the third time in a row."

Since I have just been talking about the difficulties the Americans have with their system for compiling electoral results, allow me to make a few comments concerning the many proposals to replace our electoral system with a system of proportional representation currently being discussed in Quebec, and fortunately shelved by the Trudeau government.

First of all, there is one thing that greatly displeases me in proportional representation, which is that a certain number of non-elected MPs can be named in accordance with one system or another. I abhor the idea that elected members, who have had to go down into the street to meet voters, solicit votes, and be elected by the people, will sit alongside other members who will have entered Parliament through the back door, without having taken the democratic initiative of seeking the support of the electors. Their seats would stem from organized manoeuvres on the part of officials in their party or elsewhere. What is more, citizens in the regions would still be underrepresented, because it's clear that the named members would not likely be citizens from those regions.

My friend James Bolger, who was prime minister of New Zealand from 1990 to 1997, told me one day that his greatest error as head of government was to introduce a proportional representation electoral system. He confessed to me that the system results in great political instability, and he does not appreciate the presence of members sitting in Parliament without being obliged to have themselves elected. He declared that what displeases him most is that certain elected members manipulate the apparatus of their political party in such a way that they succeed in becoming members that are appointed, and they play the same role as before without having to work to earn votes.

Take, for example the electoral situation that prevails presently in Israel. As I am writing this chapter, the Israelis are returning to the polls for the third time in twelve months, and they may soon be returning a fourth time.

Of course, our system is not perfect, but since 1867 we've had a form of parliament that has allowed us to change governments on a regular basis, at times with minority governments, that have, overall, functioned without the need for interminable negotiations to form coalitions. Knowing that our current system works quite well, why change for change's sake? I know that political science professors will disagree, because with the present system they have no chance of entering Parliament by the back door without having to get elected. As for me, having spent forty years on Parliament Hill, I've participated in a good many reforms, and I know very well that change for the sake of change does not guarantee success.

It seems obvious to me that most members are not elected with more than 50 per cent of the votes in their riding, but the system functions equally well for all parties, and all candidates are obliged to run electoral campaigns for themselves, and to represent the people they have met. The "experts" propose various solutions, each more complicated than the next. In my opinion, the easiest change and the one that produces stable governments, non-minority, and gives the voters a chance to reflect before making a final decision, is that of France: a two-ballot system. If none of the candidates obtains 50 per cent of the votes, the voters go to the polls a second time two weeks later and choose between the two candidates that have received the most support the first time around. During the two-week hiatus, the citizens have a chance to review the programs and the personalities, to take a closer look before choosing the future government, and when the process is over, each member will have received more than 50 per cent of the votes, most often producing majority governments. At the end of the mandate, when the opportunity to vote returns, the voter will know clearly whom to blame or to applaud. Since the French have adopted this system, they have not, as in the past, had governments that repeatedly fall, as in Italy and Israel.

At the time of the Fourth Republic in France, the political instability was such that it was regularly the butt of good jokes. One day, Maurice Duplessis hosted France's Prime Minister Pierre Mendès-France at the national assembly. After an hour of discussion, Duplessis said to Mendès-France, "Do you realize that we've been talking for more than an hour?" "Why, Monsieur Duplessis, are you asking me that question?" replied Mendès-France. Our dear Maurice answered, "It's because I'm wondering if you're still prime minister!"

26

THE PURE AND THE IMPURE

A s I've already said, after the 1980 federal election that brought Pierre Elliott Trudeau back to power, the prime minister gave me the responsibility of representing the federal Liberals on the No referendum committee presided over by the Quebec Liberal Party leader Claude Ryan. And so I spent five weeks on the road with the No team, and I could tell you pages and pages of stories about that, but I remember one in particular that shows how chance can sometimes guide our destiny.

It was decided that Prime Minister Trudeau would make only three appearances during the entire campaign, in order to maximize the impact of each one. As the referendum law stipulated that the leader of the No camp had to be the leader of the Quebec Liberal Party, the role of the Canadian prime minister was restricted, but the desire to know his thoughts was no less deep. On the contrary, everyone was eager to hear from him. On May 14, 1980, in Montreal, where he was to speak at the Centre Paul-Sauvé, all were on edge awaiting this historic moment. Earlier in the day, Trudeau had invited me to lunch in order to discuss what he was planning to say to the crowd that night. And so I left my office on the Hill for 24 Sussex at 11:50. Along the way, the radio was tuned to Radio-Canada, and at 11:55 it was reported on the news that René Lévesque had declared that Trudeau was not a true French Canadian or Québécois, because his Scottish blood was thicker than his French blood. A few days earlier, one of the prominent campaigners for the Yes side had spoken in the same vein of the "pure" and the "impure."

As I sat down at the table, I said to the prime minister, "You, Trudeau, are an impure; me, I'm a pure," and I went on to explain to him what I'd just heard on the radio regarding his French blood and his Scottish blood. He went pale. I believe it was at that very moment that he received the impulse that would inspire that night's speech, the greatest of his life. Later on during that lunch, he advanced the idea of declaring that if the Yes won, all the Quebec Liberal members sitting in Ottawa would resign in a bloc. I replied that that was easy for him to say, as he was approaching retirement age, but for a forty-six-year-old MP, it was more complicated.

After telling him that I was joking and that I could make a very good living outside of politics, I confirmed that it was a brilliant idea, and that it would have a strong impact on the electorate. Sometimes chance plays a large role, and if I had not heard the Radio-Canada news at 11:55 on my way to the prime minister's residence, that extremely moving section of his speech, delivered only six days before the historic vote, would likely not have existed. I invite you to read an extract:

So then, one must say, leaving that whole convoluted question aside, one must say No to ambiguity. One must say No to tricks. One must say No to contempt, because they have come to that.

I was told that no more than two days ago, Mr. Lévesque was saying that part of my name was Elliott and, since Elliott was an English name, it was perfectly understandable that I was for the No side, because, really, you see, I was not as much of a Quebecer as those who are going to vote Yes.

That, my dear friends, is what contempt is. It means saying that there are different kinds of Quebecers. It means that saying that the Quebecers on the No side are not as good Quebecers as the others and perhaps they have a drop or two of foreign blood, while the people on the Yes side have pure blood in their veins. That is what contempt is and that is the kind of division which builds up within a people, and that is what we are saying No to.

Of course my name is Pierre Elliott Trudeau. Yes, Elliott was my mother's name. It was the name borne by the Elliotts who came to Canada more than two hundred years ago. It is the name of the Elliotts who, more than one hundred years ago, settled in Saint-Gabriel-de-Brandon, where you can still see their graves in the cemetery. That is what the Elliotts are.

My name is a Québec name, but my name is a Canadian name also, and that's the story of my name.

Since Mr. Lévesque has chosen to analyze my name, let me show you how ridiculous it is to use that kind of contemptuous argument.

Mr. Pierre-Marc Johnson is a minister. Now, I ask you, is Johnson an English name or a French name?

And Louis O'Neill, a former minister of Mr. Lévesque's, and Robert Burns, and Daniel Johnson—I ask you, are they Quebecers, yes or no?

And, if we are looking at names, I saw in yesterday's newspaper that the leader of Quebec's Inuit, the Eskimos, they are going to vote No. Do you know what the leader's name is? His name is Charlie Watt. Is Charlie Watt not a Quebecer? These people have lived in Quebec since the Stone Age; they have been here since time immemorial. And Mr. Watt is not a Quebecer?

And, according to yesterday's newspaper, the chief of the Micmac Band at Restigouche, the chief of fifteen hundred Indians—what is his name? Ron Maloney. Is he not a Quebecer? The Indians have been there for a good two thousand years. And their chief is not a Quebecer?

My dear friends, Laurier said something in 1889, nearly one hundred years ago now, and it is worth taking the time to read these lines: 'My countrymen,' said Laurier, 'are not only those in whose veins runs the blood of France. My countrymen are all those people—no matter what their race or language—whom the fortunes of war, the twists and turns of fate, or their own choice, have brought among us.'*

Today, I find myself fortunate to have been able to provoke Trudeau, telling him that he was "an impure," without which he would likely not have been driven to voice the eloquent arguments you have just read.

My participation as Trudeau's responsible minister during the 1980 referendum and my later experience as prime minister of Canada during the second referendum in 1995 led to my being consulted on a number of occasions by British authorities on this subject. In 1998, British Prime Minister Tony Blair, on an official visit to Canada, asked my opinion regarding the devolution he was planning to present to his Parliament, which he hoped would satisfy the demands of Scottish nationalists. He was, like me, dealing with a territory that was making demands, in my case, Quebec, and in his, Scotland. He was not very happy when I advised him to be prudent, because my experience showed that there is no end to devolution, that what he was proposing would only be a stepping stone leading to more demands, and that it would all end with a referendum on Scottish independence. He seemed not to believe me.

On another occasion, I expressed the same opinions during a visit to my office by Gordon Brown, chancellor of the

---

* Source: Pierre Elliott Trudeau, *Transcript of a speech given by the Right Honourable Pierre Elliott Trudeau at the Paul Sauvé Arena in Montreal on May 14, 1980* (Ottawa: Office of the Prime Minister, 1980), p.15.

exchequer in Blair's cabinet, as well as an elected member from Scotland. In my exchanges with Blair and Brown, I always kept in mind the friendly discussion I'd had with Claude Charron in Vancouver during the constitutional negotiations of 1980 that followed the first Quebec referendum. I'd told Charron that I thought we could come to an agreement that would be well-received in Quebec if we all put some water in our wine, and he replied that I was wasting my time with these negotiations, because the Quebec government would never sign an agreement to repatriate a new constitution. "Remember, Jean, that clause number one of our program is to achieve the independence of Quebec, so it is impossible to sign a new Canadian constitution." I had not convinced Blair, nor Brown, that the road of devolution leads inexorably to a referendum on separation, but that is what occurred in Scotland.

Ironically, when the referendum on Scottish independence was being planned, the responsible ministers in the British government were moved to consult me twice in Canada and twice in London. I recommended two things: first, devise a clear question on separation, which they did, and second, decree that it would require a significant majority, because you don't break up a country with a majority of just a few votes.

In 1995, when Quebec Premier Jacques Parizeau officially proclaimed the holding of a second referendum, many people advised telling him that there had already been a referendum in 1980 and the case was closed. That's what is now happening in Great Britain, where Prime Minister Boris

Johnson has declared that he will not permit Scotland to hold a new referendum, because for him the matter is settled, period. I'm not sure he will be able to maintain that position. As for us, there was a second referendum in 1995, and twenty-five years later, the Parti Québécois is talking about a third. The population, however, has indicated that it's not something they want and that the idea of holding consultations on the same subject *ad vitam aeternam* is ridiculous. You have to look at what happened in Catalonia, where after there was a vote to separate from Spain, no country wanted to recognize the Catalan proclamation of independence. This would be food for thought for Quebecers if ever the *Péquistes* want to start all over again.

27

MY FRIEND "LE PIC"

O ur "politically correct" times often inspire a certain intransigence on the part of some journalists and other right-thinking observers alert to the slightest whiff of scandal—to the point where, if by chance someone appears on the political landscape with even a distant criminal record, their exclusion from the democratic process is demanded at once. But is there no possible rehabilitation after a youthful failing? Here are two examples I've known that prove the contrary.

At the time of my first election as leader of the Liberal Party of Canada in 1993, the Liberals in the riding of Oshawa, Ontario, chose Ivan Grose as their candidate. A few days later, the Toronto newspapers revealed that Grose had a criminal record incurred at the age of twenty-nine, which had earned him an eighteen-month prison sentence and made him, according to them, ineligible. But to be the candidate of a recognized party, what is required, essentially, is the approval of the party leader. Several of my advisers recommended that I reject his candidacy to avoid a controversy that might harm us during the electoral campaign. I rejected their advice and accepted Ivan Grose as the Liberal candidate in the Oshawa riding for the election on October 25, 1993. As far as I was concerned, he had paid his debt to society and deserved the right to be a citizen in every sense, and I endorsed the desire of the riding's Liberal association members to make him their representative and my candidate.

He was elected easily. At the following election, on June 2, 1997, he was again my candidate, easily re-elected. Between then and the time of my last election on November 27, 2000, we had become friends; he won a third clear victory in a row. From 1993 to 2004, Ivan Grose was a model MP, always present in the House of Commons, on committees, and in caucus. His contributions were economical, clear, intelligent, and well-received by his colleagues. In his Oshawa riding, the citizens and civil authorities appreciated his diligence and his availability. He performed the duties of parliamentary secretary and House of Commons committee chairman in exemplary fashion. I never heard any unfavourable comments concerning him during the three mandates he served as Oshawa MP. Every time I needed him, he replied, "Present."

His wife, Beverley, was assuredly the most devoted of parliamentary spouses. During the ten years when I was prime minister, during almost all of my public visits in the Toronto region, she was present, and most often helped organize the meeting when it was a Liberal Party event. I never met a person as grateful as this lady for what I was able to do for her husband.

During the 2004 election, the organizers of the Martin group took steps to reject the candidacy of Ivan Grose, the Liberal candidate who had won the Oshawa riding three times running, in order to replace him with one of their own. Then what was bound to happen, happened: instead of keeping the riding in the Liberal family, my friend Ivan's replacement came in third, behind the Conservatives and the New Democrats.

When Ivan became an Oshawa MP during my first election as prime minister, he was the first member elected under the Liberal banner in this riding for forty-seven years. Since his retirement, there have been six federal elections, and the Liberals have never won the riding back. In seventy-three years, the Liberals have only represented Oshawa for ten, with the MP Ivan Grose, whom today I salute with deep feeling.

On another occasion, when I was a lawyer in Shawinigan before becoming an MP, I had the opportunity to acquire a woodland giving onto Lac des Piles to the west. I kept it until my retirement from politics. After 2004, I decided to sell those lands bordering the lake, but to make them more attractive I wanted to build a one-kilometre road leading down to the shore. Someone recommended an entrepreneur who could do the work, and that's how I met Normand Blais, nicknamed "Le Pic."

After having completed the contract negotiations for building the road, he told me that he was happy to do the work for a former prime minister, but he felt obliged to reveal that he had a criminal record. He also indicated that he would understand my not wanting to hire him in light of that information. I asked him what he had done, and he replied that many years earlier, he had had to pay a large fine because he had "thrown a punch" at a guy in a tavern and used excessive force. I replied that he had done his duty and paid his debt to society. I thanked him for his frankness and told him in jest to think twice before coming at me, because I would give him the "Shawinigan handshake," alluding to the event on February 15, 1996, when I had seized a demonstrator by the throat. That is how the bodyguards of the Royal Canadian Mounted Police had baptised the incident.

And so this dear Normand Blais undertook the work that had to be done in the forest to reach the lake, which gave me the chance to spend some hours with this son of a trapper-guide, who knew the forest like no one else, and to learn a tremendous amount about the trees, the vegetation, fishing, trapping, hunting, and so on. He was born in Saint-Mathieu, which became Saint-Mathieu-du-Parc in 1998. Like his father, he worked in the woods year-round. His mother served them only food from the wild: the meat of moose, deer, bear, porcupine, muskrat; fish such as trout, doré, pike, bass, eel; wild strawberries, raspberries, and blueberries that were much better, obviously, than what you buy at the grocery store. He told me what to do if you get lost in the forest, and how the old-timers laid out property lines by marking trees. Often, when our visits to the land were over, we went for a beer in the very old lumber camp, still furnished with the same beds and chairs as in the time of those valiant labourers who spent months cutting wood to feed the Mauricie paper mills.

Even though the work he did for me has been completed for ten years, from time to time, when I'm at my house at Lac des Piles, near Shawinigan, I call Normand, or better, "Le Pic," and we get together on the wide veranda of his old lumber camp. We sit on the hundred-year-old chairs, some of them rocking chairs, where the lumberjacks relaxed after a hard day's work, many of them lighting pipes, enjoying a well-deserved rest. We have at our feet this beautiful Maurician forest, with its firs and other softwoods and its hardwoods, notably maple and oak, an impressive diversity that is a joy to contemplate.

Last week, Saturday, January 11, 2020, I received a phone call from the great Normand. He wished me a happy birthday, and told me he was with his parents and his father wanted to talk to me. And so this ninety-four-year-old gentleman, who had already declared that he'd always voted for me, took the phone to say, "Happy birthday, Ti-Jean!" You know, for me who has had a distinguished career, to still be called Ti-Jean by a venerable coureur de bois who voted for me for the first time in 1963, fifty-seven years ago, this was my very best birthday present. During my entire career, I wanted to be close to the people who are called "ordinary," but who are, in fact, often extraordinary. And so to hear my youthful nickname used by one of them, one of my supporters from very early in my public life, was for me a very moving moment.

You know, as I do, that many people active in public life would not have wanted to have dealings with these two friends, because of a mistake they made in their young lives. In today's fragmented societies, it's very popular in right-wing political parties to be pitiless when it comes to those who have sinned against society. This mentality is more common in the United States than in Canada. But in fact, this extremely punitive policy has never reduced the rate of criminality that exists south of our border—on the contrary. The moderation that exists in Canada has always given better results. So a second chance? Why not?

28

THE NOTWITHSTANDING CLAUSE

When Pierre Elliott Trudeau was re-elected prime minister of Canada on February 18, 1980, at the expense of Joe Clark, he entrusted me, against my will, with the responsibility for the Quebec referendum scheduled for May 20, 1980, the repatriation of the constitution, and the preparation for the Charter of Rights and Freedoms, naming me minister of justice and attorney general of Canada. And so I spent five weeks on the roads of Quebec with Claude Ryan, leader of the Quebec Liberal Party and president of the No committee, with me as vice president. The morning following the referendum, Trudeau asked me to repack my suitcases and visit each of the provincial capitals to open a dialogue concerning the repatriation of the Constitution, to be associated with a Charter of Rights and Freedoms for all Canadian citizens.

Thus, less than forty-eight hours after the No victory in Quebec, there I was on my way to meet all the provincial premiers, except for the premier of Quebec, René Lévesque, who refused to see me. You can imagine my adventures during that summer I spent with the federal delegations and those of all the other provinces. From June to September, we criss-crossed the country, with our experts and a diligent press corps, to work out a compromise that would endow us with a Charter of Rights and Freedoms applicable to every citizen of all the provinces and all the northern territories, plus, at long last, our own Constitution, a truly Canadian document to replace an old law declared by a foreign country.

When I talk of this period in my political life, probably the most difficult of my career, observers ask me if in those complex times, a true turning point in the political engagement of Pierre Elliott Trudeau, there were episodes of conflict between him, the prime minister, and me, his executor. I must say that things were relatively easy, and that he was a boss who was accessible, deeply involved, and an effective collaborator. The only two difficulties involved the inclusion of the derogation—the notorious notwithstanding clause—and the inclusion of education in both official languages in the Charter of Rights.

People are surprised that we had trouble incorporating in the Charter this right to education for all Canadians in one or the other official language. It has to be understood that Prime Minister Trudeau had clearly promised all the premiers that the repatriation of the Constitution would not affect the balance of powers between the federal government and the provinces. This explains his refusal to touch education, which was clearly under provincial jurisdiction, as set out in the 1867 British North America Act, which served as our Constitution until 1982. He felt that to recognize the right of individuals to have a French school in the nine other provinces and an English school in Quebec would be to interfere in the realm of education, thus breaking the promise not to alter the balance of powers between the federal government and the provinces. I told him that this was not an interference in provincial jurisdiction, since the Charter gave Canadian citizens the right to receive their education in English or French. However, ultimately it was up to the provinces, as part and parcel of their responsibilities for education, to put in place this new obligation devolving from the Charter of Rights and Freedoms.

When, at the very end of the process, Trudeau authorized me to include this new obligation for the provinces, I was surprised to see such little resistance on their part. I believe they understood that it was the thing to do, but they preferred to be forced to do so by a Charter obligation than by their own initiative. For a province with an English-speaking majority, the idea of including a right to education in French in a political program would not be popular, and I must say that it was probably the same thing in reverse for the Quebec delegation when it came to education in English. For me, it was a great victory.

It was far more complicated to convince the provinces that the inclusion of the derogation, the notorious notwithstanding clause, in the Charter of Rights and Freedoms was absolutely necessary if we wanted to proceed. It has to be understood that the provincial governments were not all enthusiastic about the idea of a charter that, in accordance with individual rights in Canada, found itself limiting the freedom of action of every government. In principle, the Charter was popular, but when the experts began to see how it was going to complicate the drawing up of provincial laws, my task suddenly became much more difficult. Several individuals began to argue that the Charter would, in the end, result in a governance by judges.

Even if everyone recognized that in Canada, we have an excellent separation of powers, both legislative and judiciary, some foresaw that one day we might find ourselves like the United States, where there is an extremely politicized Supreme Court, to the point where a judge is labelled either Republican or Democrat. Some asserted that in the end, it was for the elected to decide and not those named by them. Look, they said, in the United States, the Supreme Court decreed that you could not de facto limit electoral contributions, and so on. For Trudeau, it was fundamental that, as its name indicates, the Supreme Court be truly the instance of final recourse in order to protect human rights from the caprices of the political class. As for me, I was stuck between both sides. The federal government and the provinces were hunkered down in their positions, so the compromise proposed was the notwithstanding clause, which I promised the provincial delegates I would try to sell to Pierre Elliott Trudeau. A difficult task, if there ever was one . . .

Of what use is a derogation clause? Section 33 of the Charter, known as the notwithstanding clause, allows governments to shield their laws from certain applications of the Charter, except those affecting democratic rights, rights of mobility, and linguistic rights. Since 1982, the federal government has not invoked the notwithstanding clause, while provincial governments have done so a few times. From 1982 to 1985, Quebec invoked the clause in symbolic fashion in all its legislation, but it was only in 1988 that Robert Bourassa's Liberal government actually used it to apply Law 178, limiting the use of English on signs, which constitutes a limitation on liberty of expression, according to the Charter.

When a government uses Section 33 of the Charter, the derogation is not valid after five years and must be renewed. In 1993, instead of renewing the notwithstanding clause, the government of Quebec adopted Bill 66, which conformed with the Charter and rendered its renewal useless. Since 1982, four other provinces and one territory have used the notwithstanding clause, but none of these bills has been renewed after a period of five years. Which is to say that the notwithstanding clause has virtually never been invoked, or very little. That's why, during the debate on Bill 27, banning the wearing of religious symbols, I was frustrated to read the journalistic commentaries affirming that the notwithstanding clause is frequently used, because it's not true. In 2019, during the debate in Quebec on the law forbidding the wearing of religious symbols, there was no law, either federal or provincial, applying the famous clause.

A few months ago, the François Legault government signalled its intention to use the notwithstanding clause if the law banning the wearing of religious symbols were contested, which sparked a great debate across the country, where the uselessness of this legislation is well understood. When classes began in September 2020, there were only a few cases where teachers were affected. And so why attract so much negative publicity to resolve a problem that doesn't really exist? Ironically, the leader of the New Democratic Party, Jagmeet Singh, who wears a turban, could become prime minister, but he could not teach English in Montreal.

If we push the logic to the extreme, we end up in a ridiculous situation where, as has recently been the case in the South of France, rules have been adopted to forbid Muslim women from going swimming when dressed from head to toe, while other women are bathing naked on nudist beaches.

After 1982, whenever I met Pierre Elliott Trudeau, he rarely missed an opportunity to express his frustration at having been forced to accept Section 33, the so-called notwithstanding clause of the Charter, and always tendered me a gentle reproach. I replied that the federal government would have great difficulty resorting to it, and therefore the provinces could not casually do so, either.

Today, forty years after the Canadian Charter of Rights and Freedoms was added to the Constitution, there is only a single law incorporating the notwithstanding clause: the Quebec government law banning the wearing of religious symbols, and no legislation has prolonged its use beyond the five-year period. The compromise we agreed to in 1982 did not significantly alter that object of pride that is the legislative jewel in Pierre Elliott Trudeau's crown, the Canadian Charter of Rights and Freedoms.

29

2020

It's January 1, 2020, and I've finished a walk of over an hour in a temperature of minus three degrees Celsius under a cloudless sky and a sun that warms us and whose reflection on the freshly fallen snow is blinding. Forty centimetres have fallen on the shore of Lac des Piles, and the trees are slumping under the weight of the snow. I believe that there is no better way to begin the new year, and I'm sorry for all the Canadians who go south to flee winter and so miss this spectacle of amazing beauty, and this cold that gives you energy and the desire to be active and productive. That is why, even though this first day of the year is supposed to be a day of rest, I am again picking up my pen to converse with you.

I have just finished reading a book that interested me greatly, by the British journalist Steve Richards, entitled *The Prime Ministers: Reflections on Leadership from Wilson to May*. This work covers the period from 1963 to today, or the same period in which I was involved in Canadian politics, under the same political regime, in which you are successively an MP, minister, party leader, and eventually prime minister. Reading about all these career politicians who began as backbench MPs and climbed all the rungs—from being a critic on the opposition benches, to a government minister, to party leader, and finally to head of government— I realize that political life is much more complicated than I thought. Never mind their political philosophies, all these people were motivated by a single and unique preoccupation, that of making changes to better the lives of their fellow citizens and of their country, but it was not easy for any of them. I see that each of these nine prime ministers began their career on the backbenches and had to serve as simple members of Parliament for many years before becoming ministers.

When they became leaders of their party and of the British government, their hopes were high, sometimes excessively so. Some knew great success, like Margaret Thatcher and Tony Blair. Others experienced great difficulties, like Edward Heath and Gordon Brown. Still others survived their mandates relatively unscathed, like Harold Wilson, James Callaghan, and John Major. On the other hand, Margaret Thatcher and Tony Blair ended theirs in humiliating fashion, undeserved.

After having won three elections and become the star of the international right, Thatcher was summarily shown the door by her party caucus, something from which she never recovered. As for Tony Blair, after having been the emblem of modernity during the 1990s and then at the beginning of the new millennium, his error in judgment in involving his nation in the Iraq war made him *persona non grata* in his own country. When he published his memoirs, he could not even sign his book in bookstores, because there were too many protesters. He himself admitted that he preferred to be in a foreign country rather than in his own. Having known him well, I insist on saying that he did not deserve this treatment. In fact, he was one of the great politicians of his generation.

On the other hand, Edward Heath and Gordon Brown assumed the leadership of their party with, in principle, all they needed to succeed. But the great hopes they each harboured were transformed into resounding failures. Great Britain's status as a member state in the European Union was a contentious issue on the political stage for the last fifty years. David Cameron's decision to hold a referendum on Great Britain's exit from the union—Brexit—put a quick end to his political career, and his successor, Theresa May, was not able to repair the damage. She also had to leave the prime minister's residence, 10 Downing Street, with tears in her eyes. Two other British prime ministers, the Conservative John Major and the Labour Party's James Callaghan, did not serve for long. Both were seen as moderates within their parties, and they departed honourably and with a certain elegance, even if it was after an electoral defeat. Both had become prime minister after years of hard work within their party and the government. As for Harold Wilson, he was the one who survived longest as leader of the Labour Party, lasting sixteen years. He won three elections and lost one. Being leader of the Labour Party seemed an impossible task.

But despite the day-to-day political turbulence, which would have discouraged many others, the imperturbable Wilson is the one who lasted longest. It was said at the time that if an atomic bomb exploded in London, Harold Wilson would have floated on the cloud.

I spent hours immersed in reading about the evolution of a country searching for itself after the end of the Second World War and the loss of the British Empire; a country that was never able to connect with Europe; a country that wanted the benefits of the European Union without having to follow its rules; a country always seeking a special status, keeping its currency, for example; a country that struggled with Europe for sixty years and ended up sinking into the swamp of Brexit. In the end, I have come to the conclusion that Canada, which has the same political system, has survived rather well, despite the existential crises simmering away in Quebec and Alberta.

As for me, after forty years of public life, twelve elections as an MP, plus twenty years as a minister and leader of the Opposition, plus ten years as prime minister at the head of three successive majority governments, when I compare myself to my British counterparts, I find that I had an easy time of it, even if I knew two referendums, inherited public finances that were in tatters in 1993, resisted the pressure to involve the country in the Iraq war, and so on. When I think of all that, which I know better than anyone, I wonder how I was able to survive for so long. It's a mystery for historians to puzzle out.

At this, the dawn of 2020, I ask myself how our British and Canadian prime ministers will handle the complex situations in which they find themselves. With the departure of Great Britain from the European Union, the inevitable self-inflicted harm being done to the country's economy will be very difficult for Prime Minister Boris Johnson to assuage. The Europeans will probably not make too many difficulties, because they're tired of the British "maybe yes, maybe no" that has gone on for sixty years. There are certainly many among them who will simply say, "Good riddance." On the other hand, Britain will probably have the same problem as Spain when the Scots want to fly the coop. Scotland could become a second Catalonia. Also, will Northern Ireland, which does not want to leave Europe, choose to unite again with the rest of Ireland? Election days are always euphoric, but sometimes the honeymoons do not last for long.

As for Prime Minister Justin Trudeau, I think he will have an easier time than we think, even if he was lucky to retain power in the October 21 election, given that the results of the vote were less than encouraging. When we talked after the election, I told him that I envied him because I never had the opportunity to run a minority government. "That's real politics!" I told him. From 1963 to 1968, Mike Pearson led two minority governments during what were probably the most productive years for the Canadian Parliament. The best of Trudeau's ministers now have four years of experience, and none of them is really controversial. The Official Opposition has no leader and the race for the Conservative leadership promises to be hotly disputed. We will see a fight to the death between the reformists like Stephen Harper, who will want to keep control of the party, and the progressive conservatives, who will want to wrench control from the extreme right to reposition the party on the centre-right, as was the case under the governments of Joe Clark and Brian Mulroney.

As I write these lines, the Liberals must hope that Jean Charest will decide to prolong his successful career as a business lawyer. On the other hand, the Conservatives in Ontario, Quebec, and the Maritimes hope that his love for politics will come to the fore. As for me, when I saw this young politician from Sherbrooke set foot in the House of Commons, I said to my friends, "Watch this young man; he's going to go far!" And in fact, Jean Charest did become an important figure in the political landscape. He was across from me as leader of the Progressive Conservatives in the House of Commons, and was an adversary in the 1997 federal election. I encouraged him to leave the federal scene and become leader of the Liberal Party in Quebec, and three times he served as Quebec premier. We shared the stage during the 1995 referendum. I know he's going through a difficult period during this festive season. He's thinking, "Should I return to politics, or continue the good life?" His decision will be very important for him and for the citizens of Canada. We will see!

I did not have to wait for long. Today, January 20, 2020, we know that Jean Charest has decided not to be a candidate in the race for the Conservative Party leadership. I'm happy for him and his family, and also for the Liberal Party of

Canada, my party. It's too bad for the Conservatives, because he would have been a daunting party leader. It's rare that someone so experienced is available. The Conservatives often reproached him for being a career politician, a criticism that was also levelled at me. In this regard, I invite you to read this article by a veteran Canadian political journalist, Andrew Coyne, published in the *Globe and Mail* on January 14, 2020:

> "I'm not a career politician," Erin O'Toole, MP, told a television interviewer on the weekend, adding: "I think Canada needs more doers in politics and less lifers."
>
> It seems an odd thing to say, for the thrice-elected son of a career politician—John O'Toole, who held elected office at one level or another in Ontario for more than 30 years—as he prepares for his second run at the Conservative leadership. Yet it was obviously intended, a calculated appeal to the popular prejudice that what is most desirable in a politician is that he or she be untarnished, so far as possible, by actual experience in the job.
>
> Imagine. "I'm not a career doctor," the surgeon boasts, as he prepares to remove your appendix. "I think subatomic physics needs more doers and less lifers," offers the wannabe nuclear engineer. In what other line of work do dilettantes make a virtue of their inexperience, or veterans attempt to pass as rookies?
>
> Experience in politics is not automatically to be preferred—there's a place for fresh perspectives and

unsullied ideals—but neither is it to be sneered at. What makes a "lifer" is not how long they have been in office but how little they have been doing there; a time-server is defined not by time, but servility.

A career in politics was not always considered disqualifying for a career in politics. Churchill was a career politician. So were Roosevelt and Lincoln, Gladstone and Disraeli, Macdonald and Laurier. The notion that there was a contradiction between "doers" and "lifers" would not have occurred to them: Politics was what one did with one's life, if one were ambitious and public-minded. And, like most professions, it was one at which one became better with age.

The current idea, by contrast, that politics is basically easy, a business for amateurs and ingenues—that it is possible to enter politics, indeed, at the leadership level, even as a rank beginner—is rooted in a more general decline in respect for expertise of all kinds, at least where it conflicts with our biases and prior assumptions.

This is as much true on the left as the right. The populist right may despise expertise as so much elitist flim-flam, but to the identitarian left it is increasingly irrelevant: Representation—by age, sex, race and so on—is what is on their mind. What is work experience, after all, compared with lived experience? So the United States gets Donald Trump, and we get a cabinet full of 29-year-olds overseen by a high-school teacher. Anything but "career politicians."

Perhaps I am wrong, but politics has never struck me as easy. It is hard. I don't mean this necessarily as praise: so is grave robbery. Politics is dirty work, but it is also indispensable, and is best done by those who are good at it. Few are, for politics is rare in the range of occupations it combines: psychologist, lawyer, con man, diplomat, gambler, thug.

The politician must know just when to say what; how to flatter and how to bully; how to sway the mob in public and cut a deal in private; how to compromise his principles without making compromise his only principle; how to win power but also what to do with it. They must know when to attack and when to keep quiet; when to trust their gut and when to doubt it; when to get out in front of the public and when to follow.

They must be confident but not overbearing, aggressive but not alienating, pleasant but not ingratiating. They must be as ruthless at exploiting divisions as they are inspiring in their calls to unity, a moderate who appeals to radicals and a radical who appeals to moderates and, in this country, they must do all this in two languages.

These are not the sort of thing you can just pick up on the fly. Above all, they require judgment, the kind that can only be learned, if it can be learned, at great cost in years and heartache. Indeed, merely to have survived that long is testament enough of ability. Longevity in politics is never accidental: There are too many opportunities to fall through the cracks in the ice, as Jean Chrétien once put it, every single day.

Mr. Chrétien was at one time dismissed as a lifer, if memory serves—"yesterday's man," they called him— by people whose bodies were later found in a ditch. Experience in politics not only teaches: it sifts.

30.1

POTPOURRI

During a trip I made to Moscow, President Vladimir Putin invited me to a private lunch, and when he learned that I was with my grandson Philippe, he let me know that he too was welcome. And so it was a lunch for three, and a serious conversation, but in a very relaxed atmosphere. Philippe told the Russian president that he found the room in which we found ourselves very elegant. After the lunch, the president asked Philippe if he would like to visit the Kremlin with him, and my grandson enthusiastically accepted the offer. With that, Putin guided me to the exit. I descended the stairway to my car, and from the steps, Philippe waved goodbye.

Putin's predecessor, Boris Yeltsin, had had the Kremlin redecorated, adorned with works of art, historic paintings, fine tapestries, magnificent furniture and carpets, all of inestimable value. I would have been in a lot of trouble had I dared to do as much in Ottawa, and it was clear that President Putin was proud of his predecessor's audacity. For more than half an hour,

Philippe visited the Kremlin's beautiful rooms, guided by the Russian president himself! At the end of the visit, the president said in Russian, "Philippe, I must leave you, because I have to get back to work." The interpreter translated the president's words into French, and Philippe shook the interpreter's hand, thinking that it was he who was leaving and not the president. He saw himself already in a tête-à-tête with Putin!

Still concerning the Kremlin, during a Team Canada visit to Moscow, all the provincial premiers and myself found ourselves with our Russian counterparts in a magnificent, beautifully restored Kremlin room, where the czars once reigned. Quebec was represented by Bernard Landry, who, like me, had studied at the Collège de Joliette. During the discussion, I sent him a note, saying, "It's too bad that Abbé Lanoue is not here with us to drink in the beauty of this place." Abbé Lanoue was a very learned teacher with whom both Landry and I had studied.

Later, he as premier of Quebec and I as prime minister of Canada attended a reception at the Joliette Art Museum, in the course of which Landry took out of his pocket the note I'd passed him at the large Kremlin table. And, explaining what I have just described, he read my note to the assembled crowd, lamenting the absence of this distinguished educator.

Beyond this brief shared moment, those who knew me, the unconditional defender of Canada, and Bernard Landry, one of Quebec's most militant separatists, were aware that we had crossed swords on numerous occasions. For example, when he was premier of Quebec, his government decided to refurbish Quebec City's zoo and aquarium. To finance the project, his bureaucrats requested financial help from the federal government, which was essential for the realization of the project. But there was no agreement, because, as in all other similar instances across the country, the federal officials required that a plaque draw attention to the Canadian contribution, and that the provincial officials guarantee the visibility of the Maple Leaf, our country's flag. Questioned by the press regarding the delays surrounding the project, Premier Landry declared that the stumbling block was the requirement to display the Canadian flag on the site: "Quebec has no intention of prostituting itself for a few red rags!" he declared scornfully.

I replied that we would make no exception for Monsieur Landry. He didn't budge, and so there was no agreement, and the Canadian flag never flew over the famous site, because without the federal input, the project was abandoned. "No red rag, no zoo!" I argued.

During a lunch at the residence of the French ambassador in Ottawa, French Prime Minister Jean-Pierre Raffarin, on an official visit, asked me a question concerning a demand included in the referendum clarity law according to which, in addition to there being a clear question, an 80 per cent vote in favour of a Yes was required for the result to be recognized. I replied that the federal Parliament would decide if the majority was sufficient to allow for the fracturing of the country, and that it was irresponsible to break up a country like Canada with a majority of only one vote. "And so," he asked me, "you're demanding a qualified majority and *not* 80 per cent of the vote?" "That's right," I replied. He then leaned toward his wife, who was sitting at my right and listening to our exchange, to say to her, "We've been lied to!"

One day, in Quebec City, before a well-informed audience, Bernard Landry and Eddie Goldenberg were debating the same subject. Eddie had been an indispensable adviser to me for at least thirty years, and was one of the most authoritative figures when it came to Canadian politics. In the course of the discussion, Landry launched into a diatribe against me, insisting that I was undemocratic because I claimed that it was unacceptable to break up Canada with a majority of only one vote. It's now clear that I was not wrong, when you see the confusion sown following the Brexit referendum and the weak majority in favour of leaving the European Union. Eddie replied to Landry, "When you were leader of the PQ, you indicated to the members of your party that you required a clear majority to stay on as party leader, and that if you did not obtain 80 per cent of the votes, you would resign. And so when you obtained only 76 per cent, you stepped down. Yet you say that Chrétien, then prime minister of Canada, was irresponsible in demanding a clear majority and saying that a single vote was not enough to destroy a model country like Canada." Apparently devoid of arguments, Landry reacted with rage to Goldenberg's logic!

A few days after taking power as president of the United States, George W. Bush received me at the White House for a work session. During supper, Vice President Dick Cheney asked me about Vladimir Putin, whom I'd had the opportunity to meet on a few occasions. I told him that I found the Russian leader intelligent, calm, and in full command of his dossiers. I did not feel I was in the presence of a transient politician. Cheney asked me if I was troubled by the fact that he had been part of the KGB, the Soviet spy service. I said that I'd talked about that with Putin, who confirmed that he had indeed been a member of the legendary espionage organization. In fact, after he obtained his university degree, the KGB offered him his first job, which he kept for some years before going to work at city hall in Saint Petersburg, his birthplace. Then Bush interjected, for Cheney's benefit, and in order to be fair: "Don't forget that my father was director-general of the CIA!"

Without wanting to defend Putin overmuch, I find it strange that U.S. politicians and commentators constantly reproach him for having been a spy in an East German city at a time when that part of the country was a Communist terri-tory totally under the thumb of the Soviet Union. Putin was then only a pawn at the lowest level, while George Bush Sr., former president of the United States, directed the CIA, America's famous espionage organization.

———

When I became prime minister, to avoid being out in public, Aline and I attended Mass at the convent of cloistered sisters on Sundays.

In the city of Gatineau, we loved to find ourselves in the beautiful chapel for the Sunday service and to hear the nuns singing with their gentle and inspiring voices. After the ceremony, they invited Aline and me to enter the cloister, which was very unusual, because in theory no one from outside could circulate in the building's private quarters. The forty nuns sat in the room and we conversed for thirty or forty minutes. They took advantage of the opportunity to question us on current events. I was fascinated to see how well-informed these cloistered nuns were. One day, they asked me if I could help them bring to Canada six young women from Vietnam who wanted to join the convent. It was impossible for these women to leave their country without prior authorization from the Vietnamese government.

On one of my Team Canada missions in November 1994, I decided to visit Vietnam on the way home. In fact, I was the first chief of state from the Western world to make an official visit to this country, and the Vietnamese still remember it. I was able to meet the president of Vietnam, his prime minister, and the secretary general of the Communist Party, who, in that country's political system, sometimes has more influence than the president. At each of the meetings with those three leaders, I asked them to allow the six young women to leave Vietnam so that they might come to Canada, as they wished, and live as cloistered nuns dedicated to prayer for hours and hours every day. They would pray for me and for my wife.

Finally, the Vietnamese authorities acceded to my wish, and the six young Vietnamese were able to enter the Gatineau convent, where they told me, when we went to Sunday Mass, that they did pray for me every day. Perhaps they won me indulgences from God that helped me in my work ... Who knows?

Every time I go to the Ottawa airport, among the employees of the VIP service, there is to be found a certain Bruce Thibaudeau. In the course of our friendly conversations, he told me that his parents were from Shawinigan. In talking to him, I informed him that his great-grandfather Joseph-Edmond Thibaudeau had been Shawinigan's mayor. He was also a prosperous businessman and a very colourful character known as "Thibodeau the moose." I also told young Thibaudeau that there exists a photo of his ancestor the mayor circulating on 5th Street in Shawinigan, seated in a big sleigh pulled by a moose he had tamed. I was able to obtain a copy of the photo from the Shawinigan city archives. You should have seen the surprise and incredulity of the great-grandson when he saw his ancestor proceeding along Shawinigan's main street in his sleigh drawn by a moose! Now every time I see him at the airport, I ask him, "How's Thibaudeau's moose?"

30.2

POTPOURRI

When I was taking my *cours classique*, my lack of discipline was legendary. I began my studies at the Collège de Joliette, and then was forced to change colleges three times to complete that painful eight-year odyssey at the Collège de Trois-Rivières. One day, while three young Chrétien brothers, Guy, Jean, and Michel, were boarding together at the Collège de Joliette, there occurred what was perhaps a phenomenon unprecedented anywhere in the world. At the end of the year, our report cards arrived at our home in the mail, along with a letter signed by Father Jetté, advising my parents that we were, all three of us, expelled. It concluded with the director's laconic sentence "I want no more of even one of them."

Maman hid the terrible news from Papa and went off to Joliette with Maurice, the oldest of my brothers, a surgeon who had been one of the most active volunteers at the time of the college's centenary. Together, they managed to convince

Father Jetté to take us back in September. My father was never told about his three youngest sons' adventures. But when Maman died, he found the famous letter among his papers, and the reports concerning the insubordination of his three young rebels. When Papa told me about his discovery of this improbable episode, he said, "I don't know what I would have done if I'd known about it at the time." Perhaps that would have marked the end of our studies at college, and all three of us would have become workers at the Belgo paper mill instead of being a pharmacist, like Guy, a doctor and eminent researcher, like Michel, and a lawyer and politician, like me. Marie Boisvert, what an extraordinary mother she was!

Among the legends of the Collège de Trois-Rivières, there is one that many attribute to me, even if that was not the case. The food in those colleges bore no comparison with that of a five-star hotel, and the dessert on the menu was often— too often—applesauce. One day, eight students having their meal at the same table stopped eating. The priest responsible for the dining hall then decided to serve them the same dessert, meal after meal, until they learned to respect the famous compote. One day, one of the students threw his dessert onto the floor. The supervisor arrived and angrily demanded, "Who did that?" The legend was that I cheekily replied, "Ask the applesauce; it's old enough to give you an answer!" Well, it wasn't me, but my friends like to think so.

———

A precious childhood memory. I'm the kid on the right. Standing next to me is my uncle Philippe Boisvert and my brother Guy.

The Chrétien clan.

I sometimes made fun of the Conservatives, describing them as Raspa dancers: "one step forward, one step back." On victory night, Aline and I really did the Raspa dance in Grand-Mère.

In front of the Taj Mahal, the mecca for lovers.

A romantic cruise on the famous blue Danube.

Yukon's Mount Logan, in the Kluane National Park and Reserve.

Aline and I, December 31, 1999, on Parliament Hill in Ottawa. There was no better way to close out the twentieth century.

A day of climbing in Jasper, Alberta.

Nothing can beat the cool clear water of Lac des Piles.

To celebrate my eighty-sixth birthday, I enjoyed my first freefall in a simulator, accompanied by my great-grandchild, at SkyVenture in Laval, Quebec. Original, no?

On the Colorado slopes. The two security agents accompanying us ended up in the hospital with injuries.

On my favourite lake, at slow speed . . .

On my favourite lake, at high speed!

Wayne Gretzky. I always loved relaxed encounters.

Lorne "Gump" Worsley, former goalie for the Montreal Canadiens.

The legendary Maurice Richard, at an evening gala.

Why not capitalize on a visit abroad to promote our national sport?

A basketball game improvised in a Montreal alley.

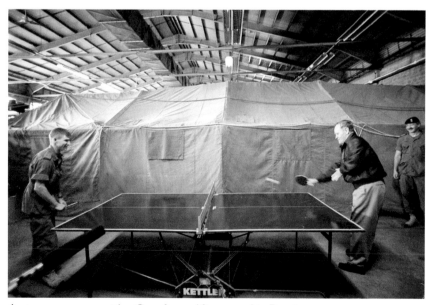

A ping pong game with a Canadian soldier posted in Bosnia.

A pause, in the middle of an election campaign, for a billiards game in Shawinigan.

The Chinese had a good laugh when they saw me hop on a bicycle. The photographers had trouble following me.

The inauguration of a hospital for those affected with leprosy, with His Eminence Cardinal Paul-Émile Léger.

A meeting with the actor Michael Douglas.

How can you not laugh when spending time with Mary Tyler Moore?

The great Canadian jazz star Diana Krall casting a spell over Ernesto Zedillo, president of Mexico.

The legendary pianist Oscar Peterson, for whom I had immense affection.

The very popular Céline Dion with her husband, René Angélil.

The immortal Charles Aznavour.

The very studious Aline.

When Pierre Elliott Trudeau left politics for good, in 1984, the favourite, by far, to replace him was John Turner. Many political figures suggested that I be a candidate, but I thought that the rule decreeing an alternation of francophone and anglophone would be a major obstacle, until suddenly Jean Marchand and Gérard Pelletier, two great friends of Pierre Trudeau, told me that it was very important that there be a francophone candidate. And they thought that I was the best-positioned from our group. Mitchell Sharp had advised me not to be a candidate if I didn't have the support of at least six ministers. In fact, seven ministers offered their support, and Pierre Elliott Trudeau told the caucus that the alternation rule didn't really exist. He added that he did not become prime minister because his father was a francophone. And the delegates had preferred him to six anglophones simply because they thought that he was the best person to lead the Liberal Party and the country. Despite that, the ascent was hard, and in the end, the informal rule of alternation played a significant role, so much so that on the second round of voting, John Turner became leader of the party and the eighteenth prime minister of Canada. You have to think that the stars were not aligned in my favour at that time.

We had managed to convince three important personalities in the party to declare their support for my candidacy a week before the opening of the leadership convention: James Sinclair, former minister of fisheries under Prime Minister Louis St. Laurent, an MP from Vancouver, and Pierre Trudeau's father-in-law; Harry Hays, former minister of agriculture, former MP, and former mayor of Calgary; and finally, Bill Benidickson, former minister of mines and resources under Mike Pearson, MP from Kenora, and member of Winnipeg's influential Richardson family. Sadly, all three of them died during the campaign for party leader. It would seem that God himself had decided that it was not yet my turn . . .

A few months ago, friends of the former prime minister John Turner organized a very nice evening on the occasion of his ninetieth birthday. Justin Trudeau, Joe Clark, and I gave little tributes at the event. Brian Mulroney and Kim Campbell did the same by video. John also gave a very nice speech, full of humour. It was certainly the first time in the history of the country that six prime ministers addressed the same audience on the same evening.

As there were many speakers, we had to keep things short. Here is what I said: "We've known each other, John and myself, for a long time. He was elected before me to Pearson's team, in 1962; I was elected as an MP the next year, in 1963. He became parliamentary secretary before me; then minister of justice before me; then finance minister before me; and Liberal Party leader before me. Then, he became prime minister after me; and finally, he's become ninety years old, still before me. Happy birthday, my friend John!"

On Tuesday, February 18, 2020, I had the pleasure of lunching with Mayor Régis Labeaume at city hall in Old Quebec, very near the former law faculty of Laval University, from which I graduated sixty-one years ago. It was a very agreeable meeting, because for someone like me, being able to talk with a politician who is fearless, like Mayor Labeaume, is a treat. When he became mayor in the wake of a by-election held when the former mayor, Andrée Boucher, suddenly died, he found himself, without any prior experience, at the helm of an important city. And so he asked Jean Pelletier, who was mayor of Quebec City for twelve years, to help him to find his sea legs. Since Pelletier was my right arm when I was leader of the Opposition and prime minister for more than ten years, we talked enthusiastically about this great public servant who was our friend. That led me to tell Labeaume about a visit that Aline, Jean Pelletier, and I had made to the majestic royal palace of Sandringham, with Queen Elizabeth, Prince Philip, and the Queen Mother.

As protocol required, I first went alone into the Queen's office, to bring her up to date on Canada's political, economic, and social situation. Her Majesty's curiosity made the meeting go on longer than predicted. During this time, in another room, Prince Philip and the Queen Mother made conversation with Aline and Pelletier. At a certain point, the Queen Mother asked Pelletier if he would like an aperitif. Jean said yes, and she asked him if he had a preference. Pelletier said, "I know that you like drinking gin; well, so do I." At once, the Queen Mother told him, "I'm going to make you a gin cocktail that I like very much." She went to the buffet and prepared two cocktails made up of a third gin, a third Campari, and a third vermouth. The Queen Mother was then ninety-eight years old, and on this occasion, she'd cut her gin with two other alcohols. You have to believe that this mixture is good for your health, as she lived a respectable 102 years. It was thanks to the Queen Mother that Jean Pelletier and I learned about this cocktail, the Negroni.

And so at the end of our lunch, Mayor Labeaume told me that at our next meeting, we would each have a Negroni in memory of our friend Jean Pelletier and the Queen Mother.

Aline and I had the pleasure of meeting the Queen Mother on a few occasions, and she often wanted to talk with us to practise speaking the language of Molière. She also informed us that she had been raised in French up to the age of five, and only then began to speak English. As for Prince Philip, part of his education had taken place in Paris, and everyone knows that the Queen speaks French. And so we sat down at the table, and during the entire meal, the conversation took place almost exclusively in French. Imagine what a pleasing moment it was for three francophones from Quebec to be at table, in a majestic royal palace in Great Britain, conversing with the Queen, the Queen Mother, and Prince Philip in our mother tongue. Political life sometimes has its good sides . . .

Aline always had a good sense of repartee, even if sometimes it could be a bit startling. One day, someone said, in her company, that my chances of winning the Liberal Party leadership in 1984 were rather slim, because of the presumed alternation rule. Her reply was scathing: "Rules like that no longer exist; the Catholic Church has just chosen a Pope who's Polish, not Italian, Jean Paul II." Her companion's jaw dropped!

On another occasion, while we were vacationing in Florida at the beginning of 2001, someone introduced me to his guests, saying that I had just been elected prime minister of Canada for the third time. As the U.S. Constitution does not allow a president to be elected more than twice, a guest blurted out, "What, is there no limit to the number of mandates in Canada?" Aline shot back, "No, but I have my own, even if it's not in the Constitution!"

At the beginning of his mandate, the new premier of Quebec, François Legault, invited me to meet with him in his office. I accepted with pleasure, and he asked me if I would agree to be consulted, given my great experience, even if we did not share the same political loyalties. I replied that I would accept with pleasure, because I thought that it was my duty to do so in the interests of the province of Quebec. We had a long and agreeable conversation, and at a certain point, he gave me a good laugh. He told me that when he was forced to change his mind, he used one of my favourite sentences: "I have to give you the same answer that Jean Chrétien did when someone insisted that he had painted himself into a corner. He'd just answered, 'Well, now I'm going to walk on the paint.'" In political life, we often believe that we've taken the right path, but then reality imposes a different reading. So we stop, admit our mistake, and put the train back on the rails. The citizens know that no one is perfect, and if sometimes you end up with paint on your shoes, you just clean them off.

When I launched my book *My Stories, My Times* in October 2018, Élizabeth Mongrain, one of the top bureaucrats at Library and Archives Canada, came to see me to ask if it was true that I had written this book on paper with a pen. I confirmed that the whole text was written by hand, as in the past. Madame Mongrain told me that I must at all costs donate my manuscript to Library and Archives Canada, because it was unbelievably priceless. I asked her why, and she told me that I would certainly be the last Canadian prime minister to write a book with a pen. And so, with pleasure, I gave her the 490 manuscript pages, all written by hand in the language of Molière.

In the parish of Baie-de-Shawinigan, there were not many families that sent their children to colleges or universities, their being too remote from our village. Very often, the neighbours told my parents that rather than make all those sacrifices to have their children study in the "big schools," it would be better to have them work in the paper mill where Papa worked. "They'll bring you money instead of making you spend it," they would say. My father replied that he'd noticed that the grass was often greener for those who had gone to university. My parents, Marie Boisvert and Wellie Chrétien, would have been very happy to hear the following anecdote.

On July 9, 2009, my younger brother, Michel, who is a famous medical researcher, phoned me to say that he was going to be named a member of the Royal Society of London, a world-renowned scientific organization. This society counts more than seventy Nobel Prize recipients among its members, and Michel was the first French Canadian to receive such a tribute. He was obviously very proud to announce this to his brother. I was very happy for him and for this well-deserved honour, because he had always worked very hard. For fifteen years, he was successively director of the Montreal Clinical Research Institute and the Loeb Health Research Institute in Ottawa while continuing to work as a researcher.

Our parents would have been in seventh heaven to see their eighteenth child become the first French Canadian to receive the Order of Merit from Queen Elizabeth and their nineteenth to be the first French Canadian to become a member of the Royal Society.

You see, it was just two days earlier that I'd learned that Her Majesty Queen Elizabeth had decided to confer on me the Order of Merit, an extremely prestigious award established in 1902, whose candidates are chosen by the sovereign herself. There are only twenty-four members in all, and since its foundation only four Canadians have received this honour:

Dr. Wilder Graves Penfield, a great medical celebrity of his time; William Lyon Mackenzie King, for his contribution to the war effort; Lester Bowles Pearson, for his Nobel Peace Prize, and I am the fourth.

As Michel was so happy, deservedly, to have been made a member of the Royal Society of London, established four hundred years ago, I didn't want to dilute his moment of pleasure, and so I did not immediately tell him that I had just received the Order of Merit. Only a week later, did I inform him of the honour Great Britain had bestowed on me two days before his own.

30.3

POTPOURRI

When the Queen Mother died, I travelled to London to represent Canada at the funeral of the woman who had been the wife of King George VI. Even though it was 2002, the authorities followed the traditional protocol of the British Empire, as it existed in the nineteenth century, which stipulates that the prime minister of a Commonwealth country has no status, as that country is officially represented by the Queen herself. And so we were grouped together as a trio, the prime minister of Canada; that of Australia, John Howard; and the prime minister of New Zealand, Helen Clark, to be driven in a bus with our spouses to the cathedral. But the most royalist of the three, John Howard, objected, and the protocol did allow us to drive to the funeral in our own cars, without, however, being allowed to display our national flags on the hoods of our vehicles, an order that was ignored. And there, at the cathedral, a surprise awaited us, because instead of entering by the main door, Australia, Canada, and

New Zealand were directed toward the right transept, and not the nave or the main aisle.

In the nave were the members of the British royal family, the members of the European royal families, with or without a kingdom, and the presidents or prime ministers of countries that are not members of the Commonwealth. Even Prime Minister Tony Blair was not in the main section. Howard, Clark, our spouses and I were to be found at the back of the right transept. John Howard, who a few months earlier had saved the monarchy in Australia, was furious; Helen Clark, a New Zealand abolitionist, laughed, and I tried to make Howard smile, saying, "We, the common folk, are on the backbenches." What was most amusing was that the rows of seats in front of us, separating us from the nave, contained members of the old English aristocracy. For the occasion, they wore vintage clothing with ermine around the neck and sleeves, prompting Aline to make John Howard grin by saying, "It smells of mothballs in here!"

After retiring temporarily from public life in 1986, I began to work in a law office with my long-time colleague Eddie Goldenberg, and I had the pleasure of receiving, as my first client, an Indigenous reserve in Northern Ontario. One day, working on the file, I had to go with Eddie to Cross Lake, in northern Manitoba, and at the end of our working day a resident of the community came to drive us to the airport, five or six kilometres from the village. On our arrival, our driver dropped us off at the door of the little building that served as an air terminal, then left immediately. As the plane had not yet arrived, we wanted to get warm inside, but the building was locked, with no sign of life within. And so we were stuck outside in the Arctic cold, wearing light coats since it was only November, and we were freezing—no laughing matter! Chilled to the bone, I asked my friend Goldenberg: "Eddie, do you know how it feels when you freeze to death?" He just replied, "No, but we're going to find out in fifteen minutes!"

During my ten years as prime minister, the political figure who impressed me most was Nelson Mandela. For me, he was the political hero of his generation the world over. Aline and I had the opportunity to meet him in South Africa, in New Zealand, in the United States, in Europe, and twice in Canada, where I had the privilege of naming him an honorary citizen of our country. Aline and I had the privilege of twice enjoying private dinners with Nelson Mandela and his charming wife, and they were among the most memorable moments of our political life. I would like to recount a memory that particularly moved me.

When President Mandela came to speak to Torontonians, who filled Maple Leaf Gardens, I organized a private meeting between the man whom I considered to be the greatest statesman of his time, and the man who was the greatest jazz musician of his generation, Oscar Peterson. It was a moment of indescribable emotion: I saw the joy on Mandela's face when he met Peterson, a leading light of his art, whose own eyes were moist in the presence of this exceptional man of peace. The tears in the eyes of my friend Oscar Peterson moved me deeply. I had taken the initiative of bringing together these two great men because I wanted to please Oscar, and I think it was a lovely surprise for the South African president at the same time.

Nelson Mandela was a person with a wonderful sense of humour. When I announced, in August 2002, that I was leaving politics after forty years of service, he sent me a message to express his unhappiness that I was retiring before the next election, because, he said, "You made me a citizen of Canada and you took away my opportunity to vote for you!"

As for Oscar Peterson, as well as being a musical superstar, he was a true gentleman. I would have liked him to become the lieutenant-governor of Ontario, but to my regret, he did not accept my proposal. One night, during a large banquet organized by the University of Ottawa, Oscar Peterson was the guest of honour. Because he was circulating in a wheel-chair, a ramp had been installed to enable him to reach the stage. When the time came for him to go up, I decided to push his wheelchair myself, at a time when I was still prime minister. Taking the microphone to make his speech, he said, "Who says you can't find good help in Canada?"

In August 1990, a few weeks after my election as leader of the Liberal Party, I left on vacation for Europe. After a visit to Italy, Aline and I, my sister Gisèle, and my brother-in-law Jacques went to Spain, where we visited the famous pilgrimage site of Santiago de Compostela. One of my friends who was a native of the region had reserved us rooms in a high-class hotel. It was a former hospital, several centuries old, that had been transformed into a magnificent hotel: from the Hospital of Catholic Kings, it became the Hotel of Catholic Kings.

My friend had informed the directors of the institution that the future prime minister of Canada would be among the arriving visitors. On the town's main square, just beside the hotel, was the famous Santiago de Compostela Cathedral, which receives thousands of visitors annually. It is, in fact, the arrival point of the pilgrims who come to visit the site, and the tomb of Saint Jacques. This magnificent cathedral has dominated the site since 1211. Even though I am not short, my brother-in-law, at six foot three, was three inches taller than me. My sister Gisèle was also very tall, which created a certain confusion when we appeared at the reception desk to receive our room keys. The hotel manager had decided to properly welcome the future prime minister and to install him in the hotel's superb royal suite.

The impressive stature and elegance of the couple Jacques and Gisèle Suzor impressed the manager to the point where he presented them with the keys to the famous suite, believing that he was dealing with a future prime minister of Canada. As for Aline and me, we were led to a room "for ordinary people." When we all met at the bar after having unpacked, Jacques and Gisèle were very excited by the huge suite they had been offered, with a view of the famous cathedral and the beautiful square. Aline and I immediately saw the error, and made them think that we too had a superb suite.

It was only the next morning that we told them that we had not spent the night in a suite, but in an ordinary room. Aline and I then went to visit the famous royal suite and saw that they were right to be impressed by such luxury. It was immense, with large windows that gave onto the square, the cathedral, and the well-preserved old town. The antique furniture was very costly, and a wooden canopy, with a sculpture of Saint Jacques, overhung the bed. Aline and I had a good laugh at the hotel manager's mistake, but we were very happy to have provided Jacques and Gisèle with such an exceptional stay.

It was our dear brother-in-law who had the last word: "The Saint Jacques cathedral was out front, above the bed was a sculpture of Saint Jacques, and Saint Jacques himself was in the bed!"

When I was leader of the Opposition, I went one day to Washington to meet some political figures, including George H. W. Bush, a few senators, our ambassador, and others. We also had on our schedule a meeting with the *Washington Post* columnists. In the course of the discussion, I was asked a number of questions about our health system. When I claimed that the Canadian public health system was effective and affordable, at an annual cost of 10 per cent of our gross national product (GNP), compared to 17 per cent of GNP expenses in the United States, a journalist advanced the opinion that the American system was much more efficient. I didn't have to reply, because one of the columnists did it for me in very convincing fashion.

He recounted that one day, he was in a Toronto hotel, when he fell ill during the night. He called the reception desk, and an ambulance appeared a few minutes later to take him to emergency in a hospital. Because the situation was urgent, he was immediately transferred to surgery to undergo an operation. Then he was installed in a recovery room. It was only after he had come to his senses that the hospital management questioned him about his history, his insurance, and so on. He said that that was not the way things went in American hospitals, and according to him, the Canadian system was superior. Since then, I've allowed myself the following little joke when I talk about the two health systems: "One of my acquaintances had a heart attack when he was on vacation in Miami. As he was leaving the hospital, they handed him a bill for the costs involved, and he had another heart attack!"

30.4

POTPOURRI

One day, Aline and I attended a reception in a private house in Ottawa, where there was a very large living room. As sometimes happens, two groups formed, one talking English, and the other French. We were with the francophone group, and Prime Minister Trudeau was talking with the guests who were expressing themselves in the language of Shakespeare. Then he moved over to greet the conversationalists speaking the language of Molière. As our group was quite animated, Trudeau said, a smile on his lips, "It seems to be more fun here than over there. What are you talking about?" I replied, "We're just back from the country, and we're talking about La Bolduc, Willie Lamothe, and the Soldier Lebrun."

Aline knew very well the tunes made popular by these artists from our Quebec youth, and she explained that she often went to visit her grandmother in the countryside, where, when night fell, an uncle took his guitar and sang the folk songs of the day for the family and neighbours. Trudeau said to Aline, "Sing one, and I'll do the same." The beseeching eyes of all those present turned toward Aline. She agreed, despite her legendary reserve, and began to sing, "Bury me on my prairie with my horse and my lasso," by Willie Lamothe. To the delight of all, and to thank her, Trudeau sang, "There's no work in Canada, a lot less in the States ..." by La Bolduc.

To help out her family, Aline worked as a secretary in a factory office in Shawinigan. First in her class, she was disappointed to have to abandon her studies so early. Later, her determination and her thirst for knowledge led her to study English, Spanish, Italian, and the piano. And when we left politics, Laurentian University in Sudbury, in Northern Ontario, made her the first chancellor of that institution of ten thousand students. She adored the role to which she dedicated herself wholeheartedly and with application for a mandate that she was, however, unable to renew. The university authorities were very disappointed to see her step down for reasons of health. As for me, I was very proud to see her perform in such exceptional fashion.

The day she was installed as chancellor, I, sitting with the graduates and their parents in the audience, was among those who heard her address, from the podium, the university community. After the ceremony, in front of a group of university professors, I said to Aline, "While we sweated it out for years in the faculties to obtain our degrees, you, Aline, were not burdened with all that fuss and bother, and as for going to university, you just came in through the front door, at the top of the institution. Bravo, Madame Chancellor!"

———

Life is not always easy for members of Parliament. The weeks are long, the days never end, and free weekends are rare. Sometimes, something unexpected can come up and take us by surprise, as occurred when I was president of the Treasury Board under Prime Minister Pierre Trudeau.

In those days, I was going back and forth between Ottawa and Shawinigan every Friday with Aline and the children, a trip that usually took eight hours. Upon arrival, I had to take part in a variety of public activities on Friday night and all day Saturday. The day after I arrived, I was in my office from 8:30 a.m. until the afternoon to receive constituents and local authorities, who wanted to meet with me. For one of the sessions, my secretary, the excellent Madame Bournival, had made an appointment for two leaders of the region's agricultural community.

The two gentlemen came into my office at the appointed hour, and after a few minutes of discussion, a hundred farmers joined them to protest against the government. When the commotion had somewhat abated, I asked the group, "Do you have an appointment?" They didn't find that very funny. So I stood up and worked my way through to the door, where a burly gentleman was blocking my way rather stubbornly. I then returned to my desk to talk only with my two invited visitors, when suddenly the phone rang. It was Prime Minister Trudeau himself on the line. When I finished the conversation with my boss, I got up and headed toward my secretary's office, saying aloud, "Who's the hammerhead who answered the phone before passing me the call? It was Trudeau on the line, and he missed the chance to tell me himself what he thought of the farmers' situation."

While talking, I was able to make my way to my secretary's office, squeezing past the protesters. Arriving in front of the individual who had appropriated Madame Bournival's place, instead of talking to him, I escaped, running out the door, and bang, found myself facing the police, whom my secretary had alerted by handing a note to another constituent, who'd also had an appointment. I must admit that despite my bravado, I was pretty nervous, trapped inside my office by a hundred angry farmers!

On March 25, 2020, when I was, like many citizens, much too becalmed at home because of the coronavirus, I received an email from John Lutz of Belleville, who wanted to talk to me about Manny McIntyre. He asked me if I knew this Black hockey player who had played for the Shawinigan Cataractes. "As you were born in 1934, you may have seen him on the ice, because he played in your town between 1945 and 1949." I phoned him to say that I did indeed know McIntyre, who had played with the Carnegie brothers, Herb and Ossie. Together, they formed an excellent trio, very popular with the spectators. Lutz told me that they were the first Blacks to play professional hockey and that there was subsequently no other trio made up of Black athletes playing at that level. He wanted to know if they'd had problems due to the colour of their skin. I replied that on the contrary, from everything I witnessed, they were greatly appreciated, and the hockey fans were very disappointed when the three left Shawinigan to play elsewhere. They were anglophones, Black, and totally welcome in a white town that was 95 per cent French-speaking: in 1945, Shawinigan, Quebec, was not Montgomery, Alabama.

In 1979, when Joe Clark was elected prime minister of Canada, he declared that he would do away with certain top bureaucrats considered, in general, too intimate with the Liberals for his liking. Now, during the electoral campaign, I stopped in Ottawa to sign some documents, and I met my excellent deputy finance minister, Bill Hood. After we'd finished our work, I asked Bill if he'd listened to the debate the day before between Prime Minister Trudeau and Leader of the Opposition Joe Clark. He replied that yes, he'd listened to it, and in his opinion, Joe had had the advantage over Pierre Elliott. I answered that I was not at all in agreement, and you had to be a Tory to draw such a conclusion. To which he responded, candidly, that he was a Conservative and had always voted for that party.

As he had indicated during the campaign, Joe Clark, once he became prime minister, wanted to divest himself of a certain number of civil servants he thought were too Liberal, and the first to receive his letter of dismissal was the deputy minister of finance, Bill Hood, who had, however, always voted Conservative.

Bill Hood's unhappiness did not last, because, since he was a very competent professional, he became number two at the International Monetary Fund in Washington after he'd been fired.

To continue in the same vein, when Brian Mulroney defeated the Liberals, led by John Turner, in 1984, he said the same thing as Joe Clark concerning the civil servants he thought too prejudiced in favour of the Liberals. But he went even further than his Conservative predecessor, targeting by name three bureaucrats: Ed Clark, who was deputy minister of finance, Robert Rabinovitch, who did the same job for the secretary of state, and Paul Tellier, my deputy minister, as I would be leaving my position as minister of energy, mines, and resources.

When Tellier saw his name in the papers, he realized that he was going to be sacked by the Mulroney government. He then shared with me his distress at having to leave the civil service and find another job, and probably having to move to another city. I asked him, "Would you like to stay in the civil service?" He replied that that was his desire, and so I told him that I thought I could help him.

I met with Minister Pat Carney, who had replaced me at the department I was leaving. I asked her what she thought of Paul Tellier, who was then her deputy minister. She replied that she had no opinion because she'd only met him once. I said that he was competent, but that I'd had a problem, because every time I met him, I couldn't help thinking that his grandfather, Sir Joseph-Mathias Tellier, was a Conservative who had been leader of the opposition in Quebec City from 1908 to 1915, and that his father, Maurice Tellier, had been president of the legislative assembly during the time of Maurice Duplessis, then leader of the Union Nationale, Quebec's de facto Conservative Party. I was able to repeat the same thing to Don Mazankowski, one of the veteran ministers in the Mulroney government.

Well, instead of showing him the door as the papers had predicted, the Conservative government named Paul Tellier clerk of the Privy Council the following week, the number one bureaucrat in the federal administration. I believe I helped Tellier to remain in the civil service in a surprising and remarkable way. He stayed in Ottawa and I never did receive any acknowledgement from him.

Poor Ed Clark was let go, but he did well in the private sector, becoming number one at the Toronto-Dominion Bank. Robert Rabinovitch also recycled himself with success. He began by making himself wealthy as one of the highly placed executives at the large Claridge investment firm, and ended his career as president of the CBC. Ed Clark and Robert Rabinovitch are both extremely grateful to Brian Mulroney for having fired them.

Still on the subject of Ed Clark: When he was a young and brilliant bureaucrat, very involved in developing policies under the Trudeau government, it was said in the business community that he was more or less Communist, because the subject of his doctoral thesis dealt with the socialist-communist system in Tanzania. But it was not mentioned that his thesis concluded that the Tanzanian Communist regime was a total failure. In the same vein, my friend Fernando Henrique Cardoso, when he was president of Brazil, told me that he'd had a lot of trouble because he was an academic recognized in several countries as an authority on Marxist ideology. Many people suggested that he had a Communist past, even though he was a centrist who participated along with Bill Clinton, Tony Blair, myself, and others in the annual informal meetings of political leaders who supported a Third Way.

30.5

POTPOURRI

I had a restaurant owner friend in Shawinigan, Paul Lamy, who moved to Victoria, British Columbia, and switched gears by taking over a twenty-room bed and breakfast. He told me that a gentleman occupied one of the rooms all year long, that he went out every afternoon to have a beer at the tavern, and that each time, he took the same bag with him. One day, my friend asked him what he was carrying around in his bag, and the man replied, "When my wife was alive, she always complained every time I went out for a beer. Well, this bag contains her ashes. Now she comes with me to the tavern every day!"

When I was prime minister, Jennifer MacIntyre, a young woman from Cape Breton, Nova Scotia, joined my team. She was a good worker and very intelligent. She also became a very young ambassador to Switzerland. Although she was an anglophone, her French was very good, and she always spoke to me in that language. One day, while we were on a working trip abroad, we arrived at an official meeting and I realized that I had forgotten my briefcase. So I asked Jennifer to go and get my *serviette* from my room. Not knowing that in French a *serviette* can also refer to a briefcase, she came back promptly with a bath towel! We had a good laugh!

At the beginning of my retirement, in 2004, in the month of February, I went to Washington to give a speech to a group of businesspeople, and the next day I was to go to Chicago for the same reason. When I arrived at Ronald Reagan Washington National Airport, I presented my diplomatic passport, on which it was written that I was the former prime minister of Canada, along with my boarding pass. The customs officer wrote a big X on my card, and I thought it meant that I was a VIP. But as I was going through electronic surveillance, a young man, six foot four and 250 pounds, grabbed me by the arms and dragged me into a little room. Then he pulled on surgical gloves and ordered me to undress, saying that he was going to inspect my lower body private parts, all this without any malicious intention; he was just doing his duty. I refused and protested vigorously. Nothing for it; prime minister of Canada or not, I had to strip naked.

Suddenly, an idea entered my head, and I took off my scarf, my winter coat, my suit jacket, my tie, my shirt, and I was just about to drop my pants, when the airport manager, whom my devoted and fast-working assistant, Bruce Hartley, had contacted, halted the procedure and apologized for the inconvenience. When he left us, I told Bruce that I had obeyed orders in order to make the following joke: as we were in the months following the Iraq war, it was doubtless George W. Bush still searching for weapons of mass destruction!

The former premier of Newfoundland Joey Smallwood, who made this British dominion part of Canadian Confederation, was a very colourful individual. When, in 1984, I became a candidate for the Liberal Party leadership, he supported me, which gave me the opportunity to see him a number of times during this period. Also, as a federal minister, I sometimes worked with him, in particular when we established Gros Morne National Park on the west coast of Newfoundland, one of the most spectacular in Canada. I could write chapters and chapters on the jokes and cunning expressions of this legendary character, but I'll confine myself to just one.

One evening, after having spent the day promoting my candidacy, as we were discussing Canadian political personalities, he said, in reference to his former colleague, the provincial premier Jean Lesage: "After having known Jean Lesage, I realized just how humble General de Gaulle was." Later, when repeating Smallwood's joke, I went on to say, "When you met Jacques Parizeau, you realized how humble

Jean Lesage was. And afterwards, when I had to work with Bernard Landry, I realized how humble Jacques Parizeau was."

In 1980, when Prime Minister Trudeau entrusted me, as minister of justice, with the task of working to imbed in our Constitution a Charter of Rights and Freedoms, I chose to provide in my speeches examples of discrimination that we had known in Canada in the past, such as the abolition of French-language education in Manitoba and Ontario. In Canada, it was only in 1916 that women obtained the right to vote, beginning in Manitoba, and we had to wait until 1940 for this right to be recognized in Quebec. Sometimes, a bit of humour helped me to communicate my message. In fact, the naked truth is sometimes hard to swallow, but sprinkled with a dash of humour, it's easier to take.

And so to show how far we'd come, I told my listeners a story about Johnny Lombardi, the son of Italian immigrants, who became a well-known and respected figure in Toronto in the field of communications. When he was young, he presented himself at the entrance to a swimming pool where you had to pay to bathe. He laid a five-cent coin down on the counter, but the employee told him that he could not go in. Johnny asked why, and the man said, "Look at the sign. What does it say?" Johnny replied, "It says 'Gentiles Only,' but I'm not Jewish; I'm Italian!" And the doorkeeper shot back, "That's worse."

———

Here is another anecdote I liked to tell: In my youth, at the Grand-Mère golf club, French Canadians could only play golf after dark. That's why I have such a big handicap!

Golf was perhaps not forbidden by the English owners, but at the time, French Canadians preferred baseball, hockey, and even lacrosse, finding the vision of adults trailing a little white ball for five hours on a beautiful July afternoon a bit silly. And to think I became a fan of this sport!

During the 1980 referendum, after one of the Yes team's leading lights talked about the pure and the impure, I, as minister and spokesperson for the federal Liberals, liked to make the crowd laugh during my speeches in Quebec by saying that Jacques Parizeau's children were impure because his wife was of Polish origin, that Claude Morin's were impure because his wife was American, and that the children of Dr. Denis Lazure were also impure because his wife too was from the United States. And so one night, in Victoriaville, a citizen called out to me from his seat, "And fat Garon is also married to an American!" As Jean Garon was a rather corpulent minister, I replied, "At least he can't say she hasn't fed him well!" During the entire referendum campaign, I made jokes of this sort every night. You can easily see why the separatists didn't like me much.

—

I spent forty years participating in political life, so it goes without saying that people ask me all sorts of questions about my experiences. Often, I explain that I consider politics as more of an art than a science. And as exciting as it is, political life can sometimes show itself to be ephemeral. I like to illustrate this idea by saying that to live a political life is like skating on thin ice. You never know when a hole is going to swallow you up and make you disappear forever. And so whenever night falls in public life, you say to yourself, "I've survived another day." Well, I survived more than 13,333 days without falling into that fateful hole.

When I was a student at the Trois-Rivières seminary, my history teacher, Abbé Hermann Plante, was very nationalist, as is still often the case in Quebec, and his courses reflected his personal convictions more than historical reality. One day, he claimed that the first francophone to become prime minister of Canada, Sir Wilfrid Laurier, was in fact an anglophone. A few years earlier, when I was a student at the Collège de Joliette, I went to Saint-Lin-Laurentides, a village situated near the town of Joliette. On that occasion, I visited the house where Sir Wilfrid Laurier was born. And so I interrupted the teacher, declaring that what he said about Laurier was false: "Laurier was born at Saint-Lin and did his classical studies at the Collège de l'Assomption. It's true that he studied law at McGill University, which is mostly anglophone, but his law practice was in Arthabaska, in the centre of Quebec, before he entered politics." Very put out by my impertinence and raising his voice, Plante said, "Chrétien, out!"

When Prime Minister Pierre Trudeau named me finance minister, what a surprise it was for me to receive a congratulatory letter from Abbé Plante himself, in which he told me that he never thought a French Canadian could one day become minister of finance in the Canadian government. "And you, even less!"

One last "potpourri": In Pierre Elliott Trudeau's cabinet, I had a colleague, Barney Danson, who had the gift of making everyone laugh. I must tell you a couple of his jokes.

In 1968, during Pierre Trudeau's first election as party leader, he was the main speaker in front of an enormous crowd gathered in Barney's riding. Three times, he wanted to mention the name of his candidate Barney Danson. Three times, his memory failed him. Once, it was "Barney Benson," another, it was "Barney Denton," and finally, "Barney Johnson." So, in front of a laughing crowd, Barney got up and interrupted Trudeau to give him his business card.

When he was minister of national defence, Barney welcomed Germany's defence minister in the capital. Passing together in front of the impressive Defence building, in the centre of Ottawa, the German minister asked Barney, "How many people work here?" Barney replied, "Half of them!"

CONCLUSION

The experience of writing my recent book, *My Stories, My Times*, and the reactions I received when it appeared were very gratifying for me. Having received so many positive comments from people of all ages, I realized that the exercise was useful, in the sense that it seems to have offered a different perspective on political life. As I had other stories to tell, I decided to pick up my pen again. There is also another personal reason that motivated me to do so.

One day, I happened to be watching a television show on the American network PBS, hosted by Maria Shriver, on the subject of growing old, and the close relationship between an active mind and a healthy body. I've always thought that you suffered more from stress if you did nothing to be active. Like everyone, I am aging (at eighty-six, I am no longer a spring chicken), and I can see the importance of managing my retirement in the most productive way possible. To write about my political and personal past is an excellent exercise in mental discipline, and I strongly recommend it. *Mens sana in corpore sano* (a healthy mind in a healthy body) is not a mantra reserved for the young; it's equally important at all ages.

In addition to the therapeutic benefits of writing, I have another goal. Politics was my life, and even though I left the arena seventeen years ago, I've maintained a great interest in public affairs, and I encourage everyone to pay attention to what is at stake in our society from day to day. I have a deep conviction that our political system can better the lives of all our fellow citizens. I wanted to continue to share my experiences and observations through this series of writings, which, I hope, shed a different light on the human dimension of political life. As well, these essays have given me the opportunity to reflect on the past, to draw lessons from it, and to face the future with optimism.

Every time I look into the rear-view mirror, I come back to the importance of the family in our society. Being of modest origins, my brothers, my sisters, and I were privileged to have had parents who raised us in exemplary fashion, with solid values as the foundation for a successful life: discipline, respect for oneself and others, a work ethic, honesty, the importance of education, generosity, and sharing. There was no better way to launch us into life.

Today, I realize how much technological change and the advent of social media have radically transformed our lives. We might have thought that all these new technologies would contribute to bringing us together. Unfortunately, in many ways, that is not always the case. I have the feeling, rather, that they cast in relief our divisions, exaggerate our disagreements, and sometimes even incite hatred. When I reflect on this subject and on the widespread opinion that our lives are being greatly bettered, I remember a remark my father made when we were watching the Montreal Canadiens on television, in black and white at the time: "They played much better on the radio!"

I am not a great practitioner of the new technologies, which sometimes make me a bit nervous. I hope that reading will continue to hold an important place in our lives, to help us to appreciate history, literature, and the arts. This new experience of the pandemic leads us to recognize even more the importance of human relationships and friendship. The quest for truth is one of the foundations on which rests the edification of our civil society and is a key component in the enlightened conduct of public debate. Unfortunately, we can see too many instances where truth is distorted and deliberate disinformation is passed on through social media, most often to the benefit of people with invidious goals.

As Marshall McLuhan said, the world has become a global village. All this great diversity creates new tensions, but also new opportunities. I firmly believe that we must embrace this diversity, and partner it with openness and tolerance as values that are essential and crucial for the flourishing of our society. Prejudices exist, of course. They are difficult to eradicate and sometimes create unbearable social tensions. But the more I age, the more I realize that we must succeed in rising above the prejudices, denounce them with vigour, speak of tolerance with conviction, and work together to make it a common and constant goal for our society. Our Charter of Rights and Freedoms constitutes the founding document on which rests Canada's social peace, and we can be proud of our capacity to celebrate diversity and to live in harmony. It's true that our history recalls to us a past that was not always exemplary, and we must continue to correct our failings. Vigilance will always be necessary, because there are always shortcomings to be addressed.

What remains? As I prepare to close this book, I want to express all the gratitude I feel toward my parents, the family I've had and in the midst of which I was raised, but above all toward Aline, my rock of Gibraltar, the love of my life. Without her unconditional support and her advice, I would not have known this remarkable career, nor the joys of a beautiful family with three children, a son-in-law, five grandchildren, and seven great-grandchildren.

I am grateful also for the education I received thanks to the sacrifices of my parents (and the more than one occasion when forgiveness was accorded me) and of a philanthropist from Grand-Mère, Monsieur Sabaton, originally from Troy, in New York State.

I feel gratitude also for the lessons I learned from practising law, that served me particularly well when Canada was invited to participate in the Iraq war. I then asserted that the proofs cited for the existence of weapons of mass destruction to justify military intervention would not have passed the test of the municipal court in Shawinigan.

I am grateful for my long stint in political life, which gave me the chance to discover the richness of my country, Canada, an incomparable land that enables us to offer, consistently, the best of lives to all our citizens. Also for having been associated with an outstanding political institution that has existed since 1867 without ever having had to change its name: the Liberal Party of Canada. I had the privilege of being its leader for thirteen years and of working with outstanding colleagues. At the same time, I was able to collaborate with representatives from the other parties in Ottawa and in the provinces in taking important initiatives for our country and internationally.

Finally, on this June 28, 2020, despite the many problems we face, it must be remembered that we have in the past, since the dawn of our nation, shown exceptional individual and collective resourcefulness in overcoming the greatest of difficulties. These will continue to serve us as we build a Canada that is prosperous and generous and that protects its own. And to inspire us in this quest for a brighter future, there are no better words than those pronounced by Sir Wilfrid Laurier more than a hundred years ago: "Faith is better than doubt. Love is better than hate."

ACKNOWLEDGEMENTS

I would like to extend my most sincere thanks to my friend Patrick Parisot, Canadian ambassador to Norway, and his spouse, Carmen Altamiro, my first readers, researchers and editors. For more than a year, with patience and generosity, they accompanied me on this new writing project.

I would also like to thank the former premier of Saskatchewan, Roy Romanow, for having agreed to write the foreword to this book. You are either a friend or you are not! As well, I thank Angèle Garceau, John Rae, Eddie Goldenberg, Alain Garceau, Bruce Hartley and Denise Labelle. They each read parts of my manuscript and offered advice, always constructive.

Finally, I would like to express my gratitude to my editors, Pierre Cayouette, Éditions La Presse, and Pamela Murray, of Random House Canada. I also thank Sheila Fischman and Donald Winkler for their excellent work in assuring the French to English translation.

A special thanks, once again, to my dear wife Aline, for her legendary support.

PHOTO CREDITS AND PERMISSIONS

All photographs by Jean-Marc Carisse / (Jean Chrétien Fonds, LAC) (Jean-Marc Carisse Fonds, LAC) and photos © Jean-Marc Carisse, with the following exceptions:

First insert: page i, top photo: Guy Nollet; bottom photo courtesy Jean Chrétien; page viii, top photo: Diana Murphy

Second insert: page i, bottom photo: Georges Gobet, AFP via Getty Images; page ii Diana Murphy / Fonds Jean Chrétien / LAC; page iv, top photo: Diana Murphy; page v, top photo: Official White House; page viii, Ottawa Sun / Tony Caldwell

Third insert: page i, top photo: courtesy Jean Chrétien; bottom photo: Jean-Pierre Karsenty, courtesy Jean Chrétien; page iii, bottom photo: Diana Murphy; page v, top left photo: courtesy Jean Chrétien; page v, bottom photo: courtesy Jean Chrétien; pages vi and vii, Pascal Rostain; page xii, Ken Bell; page xiii, top photo: Fred Chartrand

———

Grateful acknowledgment is made for permission to reprint from the following books and publications:

"Foreword to the 2015 Edition" from *Mike: The Memoirs of the Rt. Hon. Lester B. Pearson, Volume Two* by Lester B. Pearson; with a foreword by the Rt. Hon. Jean Chrétien, edited by John A. Munro and Alex I. Inglis, © University of Toronto Press 2015. Reprinted with permission of the publisher.

"In praise of career politicians: Why have voters consigned being a 'lifer' to political death?" by Andrew Coyne, 14 January 2020, © Copyright 2021 The Globe and Mail Inc. All Rights Reserved. globeandmail.com and The Globe and Mail are divisions of The Globe and Mail Inc.

Which Reminds Me by Mitchell Sharp, University of Toronto Press, 1994.

Every effort has been made to trace the copyright holders and obtain permission to reproduce quoted material. In case of any inadvertent omission, please contact the publisher.

The Rt. Hon. JEAN CHRÉTIEN was first elected to Parliament in 1963, at the age of twenty-nine. Four years later he was given his first Cabinet post and, over the next thirty years, he headed nine key ministries. From 1993 to 2003, he served as Canada's twentieth prime minister, winning three consecutive Liberal majority governments. He is the recipient of numerous honorary doctorates and is a Companion of the Order of Canada. In 2008, he became co-president of the InterAction Council, and in 2009 he was awarded the Order of Merit by Her Majesty Elizabeth II.

In 2014, he joined the law firm Dentons as counsel, working primarily in Ottawa.